Guy Spiro's Original

Astro-Weather Report

Since 1979

Pacific Time Zone Edition

January, 2007 through December, 2007

Pacific Time Zone Edition

All times in this edition are either Pacific Standard or Pacific Daylight Saving time. Daylight Saving time begins at 2:00 a.m. on the second Sunday in March, 2007, and ends at 2:00 a.m. on the first Sunday in November, 2007.

Symbols and times were produced using Astrolabe's Solar Fire® program.

© 2006 by Lightworks.com. All rights reserved. No part of this book may be reproduced in any form without permission in writing from the publisher, except by a reviewer who may quote brief passages in a review to be printed in a magazine or newspaper.

Lightworks.com
P.O. Box 1342, Morton Grove, IL 60053
www.lightworks.com
tma@lightworks.com

Printed in the United States of America

Contents

What is Astro-Weather? 5

Moon Void of Course Periods 6

Planets in Retrograde 6

Categories of Aspects Mentioned in Astro-Weather 8

Astro-Weather

    January, 2007 9

    February, 2007 22

    March, 2007 33

    April, 2007 45

    May, 2007 57

    June, 2007 69

    July, 2007 81

    August, 2007 93

    September, 2007 106

    October, 2007 118

    November, 2007 129

    December, 2007 140

A Brief Explanation of the Aspects 152

The Planets and Signs 154

Lightworks.com & The Monthly Aspectarian 156

2008 Astro-Weather Report Order Form 157

What is Astro-Weather?

Have you ever noticed that on some days you seem to run into a predominance of cheerful people, but on other days it's just the opposite? Sometimes you find that the world seems to have gone crazy, and wherever you go, someone is acting irrationally. On some days you see many more dangerous drivers than on others. There are days when it seems almost impossible to get anything done—and then it changes, and everything runs smoothly again. The general mood of the mass of people swings one way, then the other, and then sometimes back again, all seemingly with no rhyme or reason.

This is Astro-Weather.

Astro-Weather is very much like physical weather except that it operates primarily on the mental and emotional levels, which in turn influence behavior. Astro-Weather represents a new level of astrological information with which you can make more informed decisions in your daily life.

As the Moon and the planets move along their respective orbits, they form continually shifting patterns, called aspects, that signal to us the background energy in which we all function.

Astro-Weather is not sun-sign oriented. As the rain falls on the just and the unjust alike, the Astro-Weather is the context in which we all operate, whatever our sun sign happens to be. Astro-Weather transcends sun sign astrology and provides much more valuable information that anyone can use for planning and understanding the world around them.

Looking at the daily pages, you will find each day's astrological aspects, *i.e.*, energies, and the exact time of their occurrence on the margin of the page. The first and third columns' symbols are the planets involved, and the middle symbols are the angles—the aspects—that the planets are forming to each other. The text is the Astro-Weather forecast. This is my interpretation of these energies and how I think the largest number of people will see them in action. Of course, not every person will have days exactly as I describe them. But those who watch the days over a period of time will find that the patterns do show up. Different people respond to individual Astro-Weather energies differently. Just as some people like rainy days while most people do not, some people will enjoy challenging energies that most people consider to be hasslesome.

Regardless of our personal likes and dislikes, the Astro-Weather is as it is. I have described it and offer suggestions for dealing with it. I hope that you will find it as useful as I do.

Moon Void of Course Periods

The Moon is said to be void of course between the time it makes its last major aspect in a sign and its entry into the next sign. During these times, plans that are made, ideas that are had, projects that are started and major purchases almost always fall through or go wrong. This energy can be over-come, but it takes two or three times the normal amount of effort and most people most of the time will not put that much out. Please watch these times and verify this for yourself.

There is more that needs to be said about these periods, however. Moon void of course periods are among the most easily observed of astrological influences. Only a few days of watching these periods provides enough direct experience to take them seriously. A great deal of grief and frustration can be avoided by observing these periods. It should be noted that there are some positive uses for them. It is said that it is easier to break bad habits during voids of course. This is worth checking out. These periods are also good for breathing spaces in otherwise busy or hectic schedules.

As a void of course period ends when the Moon enters the next sign, it is noted that "At that point the energy will lift and general moods will tend to become more" like what the essence of that sign indicates. Aries, for instance, has at its essence an assertive and aggressive attitude, while Sagittarius tends to be more expansive and open to a wide range of ideas. This is intended as a brief reminder of the general change that occurs in the background energy at these times, depending upon the sign entered. This energy may be thought of as being similar to water in motion: It swirls aimlessly and without direction during the void of course, then becomes more focused and channeled in a particular direction when under the influence of the sign entered by the Moon. More information on these influences is given at the back of this book.

Planets in Retrograde

Mercury Retrogrades

Tuesday, February 13th through Wednesday, March 7th, 2007
Friday, June 15th through Monday, July 9th, 2007
Thursday, October 11th through Thursday, November 1st, 2007

Mercury is said to be in retrograde motion when, due to our relative orbits around the sun, parallax view causes it to appear to back up in our sky.

Mercury has rulership of communication and transportation. This affects just about everything in one way or another. When Mercury is retrograde, all things having to do with communication and transportation are prone to snafu and breakdown. You will notice during Mercury retrogrades that the incidence of computer and email problems, traffic light malfunctions, telephone service interruptions, lost and mishandled messages, general misunderstanding of information, missed connections and other problems in travel, and every other imaginable kind of trouble in these areas, rises dramatically.

Try to avoid signing legal documents, starting new projects, or opening new businesses during these periods. If it absolutely can't be avoided, then go ahead. But be aware that there will almost certainly have to be renegotiation and new beginnings at a later date, and be prepared to deal with this.

The way to handle these periods is to allow extra time for everything. Try to anticipate where problems are likely to occur and plan for dealing with them. The most important thing is to keep a good attitude. These periods occur three or four times a year for three weeks at a time. We have all lived through many of them in the past. They are annoying and frustrating, but they always pass. You may want to watch these periods for a couple weeks on either side, especially right after one of them, for the shadow to pass and the planet to pick up speed.

Venus Retrogrades

Friday, July 27th through Saturday, September 8th, 2007

The other two inner, or personal, planets are Venus and Mars. When they are retrograde there tends to be more of a noticeable effect on our personal lives. When Venus is retrograde, all things related to Venus are called into question. Relationships of all kinds, especially the romantic variety, can be more of a challenge. Perhaps the most common and potentially troublesome manifestation of this is a tendency for relationships from the past to reappear. This can sometimes take the form of the actual person showing up. More often one can fall into comparing current partners with idealized memories of past partners. Old relationship habits and ideas also tend to return. All of these things can put stress on current relationships. Those who reestablish old relationships during Venus retrogrades often remember why those relationships ended when the retrograde ends. Of course, it is within the realm of possibil-ity that the reestablishment of an old relationship is a good thing and a Venus retro is the time for that to happen. Discernment is of the utmost importance. Venus also rules such things as the arts and it is ill advised to drop a bundle on an expensive painting or other adornment during a Venus retrograde.

Mars Retrogrades

November 15th, 2007 through January 30th, 2008

When Mars is retrograde, all things related to Mars are called into question. Mars has rulership of energy, and during a retrograde there will be somewhat less of it available. Bursts of energy will be followed by longer recovery periods. During a Mars retrograde, disputes from the past have a tendency to reignite. It is unwise to rip scabs off of old wounds at these times. Mars was the God of war and its retrograde periods are not the time to start trouble. Saddam Hussein invaded Kuwait during a Mars retrograde as an example.

Outer Planet Retrogrades

The outer planets are retrograde for months at a time and the effect is not as pertinent on a day to day basis. In some unusual circumstances, their direct and retrograde motions will be mentioned in Astro-Weather, but this is rare.

Categories of the Aspects Mentioned in Astro-Weather

Because the inner planets, Mercury, Venus, and Mars are relatively close to the Sun (and therefore, to Earth), their relatively small, fast orbits allow their aspects to each other to change often. The outer planets, Jupiter, Saturn, Uranus, Neptune, and Pluto, however, move in vastly larger and slower orbits, producing aspects that remain virtually unchanged for months, years or even decades in some cases. Aspects between outer planets will usually be mentioned in the monthly overviews.

Aspects between inner planets and between inner and outer planets will be spoken of as major energies. Aspects between the Moon and the planets are generally referred to as minor energies. On days when there are one or more major energies, the minor energies are not mentioned as much; the major energies will overshadow the minor. On days with one or no major energies, the minor energies receive more attention as their effect will be more noticeable.

Pacific Time   January 2007

January 2007

Overview

As January opens, the Saturn trine Pluto that seemed to lighten things the past two months will be fading as Saturn retrogrades back from it, but we have had our first taste of the energy that signals the beginning of the end of the current international conflict that came to broad attention on 9/11 of 2001. This energy will return to peak again later this coming August with another period when the light at the end of the tunnel won't seem to be another train, but things will heat back up through January. As the month progresses, Saturn will move back toward the opposition to Neptune which we had through last August and September. This will likely reignite southern Lebanon, but it can inflame any of the theatres in the larger context. It will peak again next month and remain into early summer when it will peak again. January will be dominated by the Jupiter square Uranus that started to roll in last month. This energy will tend to exaggerate tensions and will be very large in the media. Attacks will tend to be more technological and ambitious. Jupiter's involvement will make things seem larger than they really are, and there will be silver linings to whatever does occur with this energy. Due to retrogrades, this aspect will remain with us through most of the year.

On the more personal level, the month starts off with a flurry of high energy days, not the least of which is the full Moon on the 3rd. There are many high energy days scattered through the month. The four-day weekend of the 12th is especially intense, with a great deal of major energies both positive and cautionary. The weekend of the 26th also merits extra attention. This is definitely a month to read ahead and plan for making the most of the positives and minimizing the negatives. The most significant Moon void of course periods occur on the 3rd–4th and the 30th–31st. There are a few half day voids, most notably the 9th and the 14th.

Monday, 1st – New Year's Day

♀	☌	♅	1:29
☽	△	♆	10:31
♀	⚹	♇	11:05
☽	☍	♂	12:04PM
☿	⚹	♃	9:11
☽	⚹	♄	9:25

The very strong but erratic social energy from last night will run strongly through today's predawn. Have fun, but make good choices. High energy continues today with four more major energies to deal with. The first easily brings problems to relationships, especially where erratic behavior and unrealistic demands for sudden change are indulged. The second is more positive relationship energy that is very good for communicating in relationships on deeper levels. Make good use of this, but be mindful of the first aspect. The third is very positive energy for anything involving communication and transportation. There will be much to learn today, but watch for some to get carried away. The fourth is excellent for any activity involving technology, electronic media and magic. This energy can also very easily be used socially and many will use it for fun. For those not caught up in the cautionary relationship energy, this should be an enjoyable and stimulating day.

Tuesday, 2nd

☉	⚹	♅	1:17
☽	☍	♇	2:06
☽	⚻	♀	3:34
☽	→	♋	7:14
☿	□	♄	11:12
☽	□	♆	12:50PM
☽	⚻	♃	10:34
☽	⚼	♄	11:47

The high energy from the past few days will continue through today. Reread. The Moon will be void of course this morning from 2:06 until 7:14 when it will enter Cancer. At that point the energy will lift noticeably and general moods will tend to become more sensitive and protective, and tomorrow's full Moon will roll in very strongly. There is another major energy running throughout today that can bring problems to communication and transportation, especially where people run into restriction and frustration. Watch for people acting out on this. With the right choices, much may be accomplished and positive change is possible. With the wrong choices ...

Wednesday, 3rd

☽	☍	☿	1:32
☽	△	♅	3:50
☽	☍	☉	5:57
☽	⚻	♆	3:41PM
♀	—	♒	7:32
☽	⚻	♂	8:16
☿	⚹	♅	9:20

Today is full Moon day. It is exact at 5:57 this morning. Remember that full Moons are always high energy and deserve to be approached with respect. This particular full Moon is rather more benign than many others. Unfortunately, the Moon will be void of course from 5:57 this morning well into tomorrow afternoon. Enjoy the high energy, but try not to take new things too seriously. Tend to old business. There are two more major energies running throughout today. The first indicates a general shift in relationship energy and aesthetic pursuits towards a more independent and free-thinking mode. The second is again very good for anything involving electricity, electronic media and magic. Remember the void of course.

Thursday, 4th

☽	□	♃	2:01
☽	⚻	♄	2:45
☽	□	♅	7:06
☽	#	☿	7:45
☽	⚻	♇	8:00

The long Moon void of course period runs through the morning and finally ends at 1:15 this afternoon when the Moon enters Leo. At that point the energy will lift very noticeably and general moods will tend to become more intense and concerned with self. Try to relax and take it easy

Pacific Time   January 2007

☽	─	♌	1:15PM
☽	☍	♀	3:08
☽	#	♂	3:24
☽	#	☉	8:36

through the void of course, remembering that the full Moon will remain with us very much through today, especially following the void of course. There will be a major energy building throughout the day that is very positive for making new beginnings in relationships and aesthetics. Watch for some tendency to get carried away. This energy is also very highly social and that is how most people will use it. Minor aspects are mixed and good choices will be in order.

Friday, 5th

☽	□	♂	1:33
☽	#	♀	5:33
☽	#	♃	5:41
☽	△	♃	6:15
♀	∥	♃	7:33
☽	⚻	♅	11:08PM
☽	□	♆	12:03
☽	⚻	☿	4:30
☽	⚻	☉	6:02

The high social energy mentioned yesterday peaks this morning and remains with us through tomorrow. Have fun, but try not to overindulge. There will be some people proving to themselves once again that it is possible to get too much of a good thing. Watch the early predawn for a brief period of aggressiveness. The late predawn to early morning is mixed. Take an expansive approach, but watch for minor relationship issues. Positive moods follow closely, but watch the late morning through midday for a downturn with erratic emotional responses and coercive attitudes. The late afternoon to early evening brings more irritability, and good choices will be very important. Enjoy the strong social energy, but be at least a little bit careful.

Saturday, 6th

☽	☍	♆	11:38
☽	#	♆	5:29
☽	△	♂	7:48
☽	#	♆	10:08
☽	☌	♄	10:58
☽	∥	♄	2:33PM
☽	△	♆	4:55
☉	☌	☿	10:03
☽	─	♍	10:19

Late Friday night social energy is likely to run well into today's predawn, but watch the early predawn for spaciness. There is a major energy running through the day that is very positive for looking within and coming to greater self understanding. Light will be shed in all areas and there will be much to learn. Watch the late predawn to very early morning for a brief period of coercive irritability, but this will likely pass unnoticed. Good moods should run through much of the rest of the morning and an active approach will serve best. Watch for another period of spaciness and hard attitudes in the late morning. Take a disciplined approach through the afternoon and good moods should run through the late afternoon. Be aware however that the Moon will be void of course from 4:55 this afternoon until 10:19 tonight when it will enter Virgo. At that point the energy will lift very noticeably and general moods will tend to become more discerning and concerned with detail and the social energy will shift into a higher gear.

Sunday, 7th

| ☽ | □ | ☉ | 1:38 |

The high positive energy mentioned yesterday remains with

Astro-Weather   11

January 2007   Pacific Time

☽	♉	☿	1:50
☽	⚻	♀	6:51
☽	□	♃	5:16PM
☽	#	♅	8:44
☽	☍	♅	9:37

us through today and is joined by another major aspect that is of the positive persuasion. This is very good for communication along spiritual lines. Meditate, pray, teach, learn and grow. There is another major energy coming into focus throughout the day that is excellent for any activity involving the use of energy and power. Take a disciplined approach and much may be accomplished. Watch the early predawn for general minor irritability. The very early morning chips in with erratic emotional responses in relationships. Most of the rest of the daytime opens up. The late afternoon may have a period of exaggerated emotional response, but this is likely to pass unnoticed. Watch the mid evening to late night for more minor erratic irritability.

Monday, 8th

☿	⚺	♆	12:45
♂	△	♄	10:05
☽	△	☉	10:10
☽	⚻	♆	10:45
☽	△	☿	12:19PM
☽	♉	♀	4:13
☉	⚺	♆	5:15
☽	⚺	♄	10:10
☽	□	♂	11:01

High energy from the past few days will remain very much with us through today. Make good use of the energy for getting things done in an active yet solid way. There is another major energy running throughout the day that is excellent for meditative and spiritual practices. Be open to the intuitive process. Aside from the major energy, the predawn through much of the morning is open. The late morning to midday is mixed. Watch for minor erratic spaciness, but this is likely to pass unnoticed. Good moods and positive communication will predominate. Watch the late afternoon for a very brief period of relationship issues, but this also is likely to pass unnoticed.

Tuesday, 9th

☽	□	♆	4:50
☽	—	♎	10:15
☽	♉	♆	5:10PM
☿	∥	♂	6:13

There is a major energy running throughout the day that is positive for making new beginnings involving communication, transportation and the uses of energy and power. Most of today's predawn is open, but watch the late predawn for irritability and coerciveness. Be aware that the Moon will be void of course from 4:50 this morning until 10:15 this morning when it enters Libra. At that point the energy will lift and general moods will tend to become more concerned with balance and beauty. Most of the afternoon is open to do with what you will, but you will want to watch for minor spaciness in the late afternoon. The nighttime opens up once again.

Wednesday, 10th

☽	△	♀	2:13
☽	⚹	♄	4:27
☽	⚹	♃	6:49

Most of today's predawn is open and positive. Take a friendly and cooperative approach. The late predawn may have a brief period of hard attitudes, but this will give way

☽ ⚻ ♅ 10:26
☽ // ♅ 3:32PM
☽ △ ♆ 11:46

quickly to a longer period of much more positive moods and an expansive approach will serve best. There is another brief period of erratic irritability in the late morning which returns for another short stay in the mid afternoon. Moods should be open in between times, but watch the late night for a heavier irritable and hard attitude energy to begin to roll in.

Thursday, 11th

☽ □ ☉ 4:44
☿ ⚻ ♄ 9:27
☽ ⚹ ♄ 10:46PM
☽ □ ☿ 10:59
☽ ∠ ♃ 1:47
☽ ⚹ ♂ 3:55
☽ ⚼ ♅ 4:59
☽ ⚹ ♇ 5:55
☽ – ♏ 11:07
☽ # ♄ 11:26

There is a major energy running throughout today that easily brings problems to communication and transportation especially where people run into restrictions and frustrations and have ill considered reactions. This energy can also lead to similar problems with authority and older people. Count to ten. Watch the late predawn for a period of potentially very bad moods. Minor aspects following that are mixed through the day and good choices will yield positive results. There is another major energy that will come into focus especially tonight that is very high social energy. Plan some sort of fun activity, but be aware that the Moon will be void of course from 5:55 this afternoon until 11:07 tonight when it will enter Scorpio. At that point the energy will lift and general moods will tend to become more intense.

Friday, 12th

☽ // ♆ 3:04
♀ ⚹ ♃ 4:44
☽ // ♇ 8:20
☿ ∠ ♃ 9:19
☽ ⚺ ♃ 8:21PM
☽ // ♀ 8:22
☽ □ ♀ 9:52
☽ △ ♅ 11:05
☽ ∠ ♂ 11:53

The high social energy mentioned yesterday will run very strongly through today and the partyhards will be in their glory. Have fun with this, but don't get carried away. There are two more major energies to deal with as well. The first easily brings problems to communication and transportation especially where people bite off more than they can chew. Watch as people try to say and do too much and don't make promises that will be difficult to keep. The second can be used very positively, but needs to be taken very seriously. This energy is very good for beginning projects involving energy and power on the deepest levels. Be aware of anything you set in motion today as it may have much deeper ramifications than you realize. Minor aspects are mixed at best and good choices will be needed, especially through the late night. Have fun, but be aware.

Saturday, 13th

☽ ∠ ♇ 12:00
♂ ☌ ♇ 1:57
☿ ∠ ♅ 6:42
♀ ⚺ ♅ 10:03

High energy from yesterday will continue very strongly through today. Reread and apply. It is joined by no fewer than seven major energies. The first easily brings problems to communication and transportation, especially where elec-

☽	∥	♃	10:33
☽	∥	☉	11:00
☽	□	♆	11:58
☿	⚺	♇	1:22PM
☽	∥	☿	6:27
♀	∠	♇	6:59
☉	∥	♃	8:05
☿	⚺	♂	9:50
☽	⚹	☉	9:58
☽	□	♄	10:04
☉	⚻	♄	11:07

tricity and electronic media are involved. Also watch for erratic and bizarre behavior as this is nutball energy as well. The second is positive for fun, interesting and stimulating activities in relationships. Plan something out of the ordinary, but be mindful of the day's other energies. The third is positive for looking within and coming to deeper self understanding. Keep the eyes and ears open as secrets will be revealed and there will be much to learn. The fourth easily brings about a heavy and potentially coercive sexuality. While this can be fun for some it can be unsettling and even dangerous for others. As always with this energy, protect the vulnerable. The fifth is very positive for beginnings of all kinds. This energy sheds a great deal of light and the wise will focus here. The sixth is very good for anything involving communication and transportation. Take an active approach and much may be accomplished. The seventh is rather more problematic and easily brings feelings of restriction and frustration with a tendency to act out erratically. This energy easily leads to problems with and for authority, older people and traditional matters. This is not the day to smart off around elders or authority figures. Minor aspects are mixed at best and good choices are definitely in order on this very high energy day. Have fun tonight, but by all means stay alert.

Sunday, 14th

☽	∥	♂	2:38
☽	⚺	♇	5:23
☽	⚺	♂	7:00
☽	⚹	☿	7:48
☽	→	♐	10:09
♀	∠	♂	5:58PM

High energy from yesterday will run very strongly through today. Reread the past couple of days and apply the cautions. Late Saturday night social scenes are likely to extend well into today's predawn. Again, have fun, but be careful. There is another major energy running throughout the day. This aspect easily brings problems to relationships and this is likely to be a good day to let some things go by. Those looking for trouble will find it. Don't be among them. The morning should be primarily good mood oriented, but be aware that the Moon will be void of course this morning from 7:48 until 10:09 when it will enter Sagittarius. At that point the energy will lift noticeably and general moods will tend to become more expansive and open to a wide range of ideas. Aside from the major energy, the rest of the day through the late night is open.

Monday, 15th – Martin Luther King Day

☿	→	♒	1:25
☽	∠	☉	5:07
☽	☌	♃	7:09

Fallout from the past several days is likely to linger through today at least. Don't be surprised if the intensity remains high. There is a major energy in the early predawn that indi-

Pacific Time   January 2007

☽	□	♅	9:03
☽	⚹	♀	1:56PM
☽	⚼	☿	4:23
☽	⚹	♆	9:07

cates a general shift in thinking and communicating towards a more independent and free thinking mode. Aside from the major energy, today's predawn is open. Watch the early morning for a brief period of minor irritability that is likely to pass unnoticed. Take an expansive approach through the morning, but watch the mid morning for some people to fall prey to an erratic irritability. Sidestep that energy and take a friendly and cooperative approach through the afternoon. There may be another brief period of irritability in the late afternoon, but this again will not amount to much at all. Good moods will run through the later evening and late night.

Tuesday, 16th

☽	△	♄	6:11
☽	⚻	☉	11:04
☉	⚼	♃	12:17PM
♂	—	♑	12:54
☽	☌	♆	1:27
☽	—	♑	5:48
☽	☌	♂	6:05
☽	⚼	♀	8:08
☽	⚻	☿	11:37

There are three major energies running throughout the day. The first tends to bring about feelings of positivity and well being. The problem is that people tend to get carried away with this and ego battles can sometimes result. Be careful in your dealings with authority. The second indicates a general shift in the way energy and power is used and regarded toward a more disciplined and grounded mode. The third is very good for initiating any projects involving communication and transportation and this is a go for it day. Get anything important done, however, before 1:27 this afternoon as the Moon will be void of course from then until 5:48 this afternoon when it will enter Capricorn. At that point the energy will lift and general moods will tend to become more practical and concerned with accomplishment. Take an active approach through the evening. Watch for some potential minor relationship issues and make good choices.

Wednesday, 17th

☿	∥	♃	12:02
☽	⚼	♆	12:21
☽	□	♄	8:55
☉	⚼	♅	8:56
☽	⚻	♃	2:16PM
☽	⚹	♅	3:28
☉	⚻	♇	7:04

High energy from yesterday will tend to remain with us through today. You will also notice energy levels rising throughout today as tomorrow's new Moon begins to roll in. It will be a good idea to consider the new Moon as starting today. There are two other major energies to deal with today that are somewhat paradoxical. The first brings out the crazies. Watch for erratic and bizarre behavior of all kinds. If you see someone who seems a clown or two short of a circus, they quite likely are. This energy also easily brings problems with and for authority. Watch for sudden changes and challenges. The second sheds light on things normally kept secret and hidden. This is a rather more positive aspect involving this energy, but you will still want

Astro-Weather

to guard your secrets and observe as others' are exposed. Observe and learn. Minor aspects are positive and good moods should run from the afternoon through the late night.

☽	⚺	♀	1:15
☽	⚺	♆	2:48
☽	⚻	♄	10:57
☽	∠	♃	4:39PM
☽	∠	♅	5:33
☽	⚺	♇	6:14
♀	☌	♆	6:48
☽	☌	☉	7:59
☽	∥	♂	9:17
☽	→	♒	10:14

Thursday, 18th

Today is new Moon day. It is exact at 7:59 tonight. Remember that what you start at new moon brings results at the next full Moon. It always pays to begin things now that you'd like to see the results of later. This particular new to full period is rather more benign than others we have seen. Take an expansive approach and work on deep, positive change. There's another major energy running throughout the day which is very positive for taking relationships to more spiritual levels. This energy can be used socially, however, and that, of course, is what most people will do with it. Have fun tonight, but remember the new Moon and be good. Also be aware that the Moon will be void of course tonight from 7:59 until 10:14 when it will enter Aquarius. At that point the energy will lift noticeably and general moods will tend to become more independent and free thinking.

☽	⚺	♂	1:24
♀	∥	♇	4:45
☽	☌	☿	10:55
☽	∥	♃	10:58
☽	∥	☿	5:27PM
☽	∥	☉	5:31
☽	⚹	♃	6:29
☉	∥	☿	6:45
☽	⚺	♅	7:07
☽	∠	♇	7:46

Friday, 19th

Consider the new Moon to run on through today at least and be good. There are two major energies running throughout the day. The first can be positive for initiating deep changes in relationships. There can, however, be a strong sexual component to this which has the potential to become coercive. Deal carefully in this area. The second is very good for looking within, coming to greater self understanding and initiating positive change. Light will be shed, so stay awake through this day as there is likely to be much to learn. Aside from the major energies, today's predawn should be good mood oriented and the much of the morning is open. Take a communicative and expansive approach through the late morning. The afternoon opens up again. Take an expansive approach through the evening, but watch for some potential for minor coercive irritability which may not register with most people, but you don't want to be among them. This is likely to be a high energy social Friday night, but be aware.

☉	→	♒	3:02
☽	∠	♂	4:10
☽	☌	♆	6:01

Saturday, 20th

The Sun enters the fixed air sign Aquarius at 3:02 this morning and the middle portion of the winter season begins. During this time, you will want to make plans for major

☽	☌	♀	9:17
☽	∥	♇	9:58
☽	∥	♀	12:08PM
☽	☍	♄	1:33
☽	∥	♆	2:46
☽	#	♄	4:36
☽	⚹	♇	8:59

projects to be started at the Vernal Equinox coming up in March. There is another major energy which peaks tomorrow morning, but will be coming into focus throughout today and especially tonight that definitely bears watching. While this will be perceived as high social energy, which it certainly passes for, it is highly cautionary as well. Be on the look out for problems involving water and hot and caustic liquids and gases. Be on guard against those overindulging in alcohol and other recreational substances. You will also want to watch for spacy and inebriant fueled altercations. Minor aspects are of very little help through the day and good choices will be very necessary. This will be a very high energy social Saturday night, but one to be very careful with. Also be aware that the Moon will be void of course from 8:59 tonight into tomorrow's early predawn.

Sunday, 21st

☽	→	♓	12:47
☽	⚺	☉	2:27
☽	⚹	♂	6:37
♂	∠	♆	6:03PM
☽	⚺	☿	8:01
☽	∥	♅	8:18
☽	□	♃	9:19
☽	☌	♅	9:29

Last night's Moon void of course period ends at 12:47 this morning when the Moon enters Pisces. At that point the energy will lift and general moods will tend to become somewhat more mellow if a bit spacy. The high social but cautionary energy from yesterday will remain very strongly with us through today. Reread and apply. There are two more major energies coming into focus. The first can bring about spaciness in relationships, but is best used in taking relationships to more spiritual levels. The second, however, which peaks tomorrow morning, can bring problems to relationships, especially where people indulge in feelings of restriction and frustration and act out on it. Avoid hard, cold attitudes and if trouble pops up in this realm, switch to damage control as consequences can be much more severe and longer lasting than normal. Moods should be positive from the mid predawn through the early morning, but you will want to make good choices through the rest of the day.

Monday, 22nd

♀	∥	♆	2:13
☽	∠	☉	5:22
♀	☍	♄	7:38
☿	⚹	♃	8:13
☽	⚺	♆	8:15
☿	⚺	♅	8:39
☿	∠	♇	1:41PM
♃	□	♅	1:45
☽	⚻	♄	3:22
☽	⚺	♀	4:09

The high but cautionary relationship energy mentioned yesterday will remain very much with us through today and tomorrow as well. Reread and apply. There are five other major energies today. The first two are excellent for any activity involving communication and transportation. Take an expansive, innovative approach for best results. This energy is also very good for magical pursuits and those involved in these matters should make the most of it. The third is related to the first two, but is rather more cautionary. Be careful in communication and transportation especially

January 2007   **Pacific Time**

☽	□	♇	11:10
♀	#	♄	11:44

where coercive attitudes and nasty moods are indulged. This energy also brings about the exposure of things normally kept hidden. Guard your secrets and keep the eyes and ears open as there will be much to learn. The fourth is a long range outer planet aspect mentioned in the Overview. Watch the news for activity on the international scene and in the ongoing conflict. The fifth continues the difficult relationship energy. Choose well and be aware that the Moon will be void of course from 11:10 tonight well into tomorrow's predawn.

Tuesday, 23rd

☽	∠	☿	12:26
☽	−	♈	2:52
☽	✶	☉	8:22
☽	∠	♆	9:24
☽	□	♂	11:26
☽	⊓	♄	4:21PM
☽	∠	♀	7:40
☽	⚹	♅	11:51

High energy from the past few days will tend to linger through today. Reread and apply, especially the cautionary energy involving relationships. Last night's Moon void of course ends this morning at 2:52 when the Moon enters Aries. At that point the energy will lift and general moods will tend to become more assertive and aggressive. Moods should be positive through the early morning and with a cooperative approach, much may be accomplished. Watch the mid morning for minor spaciness and the midday for a brief period of aggressive attitudes. Most of the rest of the afternoon is open, but watch the late afternoon for hard attitudes. This will pass quickly, but there may be relationship issues in the evening. Moods will improve in the late night.

Wednesday, 24th

☽	△	♃	12:10
☽	#	♅	1:53
☽	✶	☿	5:03
☽	✶	♆	10:43
☽	△	♄	5:31PM
☽	✶	♀	11:28

Today's predawn starts out with positive moods, and predawners should make the most of it. The mid predawn may have a brief period of erratic irritability, but this will pass quickly, if it is noticed at all. Good moods return in late predawn and a communicative, cooperative approach will yield the best results. Get a lot done through the morning. Take a friendly attitude through the late morning and be open to the intuitive process. Good moods should continue through the afternoon, evening, and right on into the late night. Make good choices and enjoy this day.

Thursday, 25th

☽	∠	♅	1:18
☽	△	♆	1:50
☽	⊓	♃	1:52
☽	#	♀	2:48
☽	−	♉	5:28
☽	∥	♄	6:46

Good moods from yesterday should linger into today's very early predawn, but watch for developing minor irritability that will likely pass unnoticed. The Moon will be void of course this morning from 1:50 until 5:28 when it will enter Taurus. At that point the energy will lift and general moods will tend to become more down to earth and concerned with

☽	#	♆	7:54
☽	#	♇	12:56PM
☽	#	☿	2:53
☽	□	☉	3:01
☽	△	♂	5:01
☽	#	☉	10:56

enjoyment. Take it easy through the void of course, but be prepared to get down to it as it ends. There is a major energy coming into focus throughout the day that is positive for taking relationships to deeper levels. There may be a strong sexual component to this, however, which should be handled carefully. Take a disciplined approach through the morning following the void of course, but watch for spaciness. The midday contributes a period of coercive attitudes and you will want to keep an eye on others' motives. The mid afternoon is no improvement and features argumentativeness and just plain rotten moods. Sidestep that energy and good moods may follow. Indulge in nastiness and you may miss something good.

Friday, 26th

♀	⚹	♇	2:56
☽	⚹	♅	3:02
☽	⚼	♇	3:32
☽	⚻	♃	3:49
☿	☌	♆	5:20
☿	//	♇	8:46
☽	#	♃	1:14PM
☽	□	♆	2:05
☽	□	☿	3:16
☽	⚼	♂	8:18
☽	□	♄	8:39

The high social relationship energy mentioned yesterday will remain with us through today. There are three other major energies to be aware of. The first is very positive for making new beginnings in spiritual, meditative, or prayer activities. Be open to the intuitive process. The second is much the same, but deepens the thought process. Look within and come to greater self understanding. Also keep the eyes and ears open as things that are normally less visible will be more apparent. Much may be learned. The third is much more cautionary in nature. Watch for people running up against restrictions and frustrations which in extreme cases can lead to violence. Also watch anything involving the expenditure of energy and power. Deal carefully with this aspect as consequences to running afoul of it can be harsher and longer lasting than usual. Minor aspects are of little to no help through the day and good choices are highly recommended. This may not be the most positive, social Friday night you've ever encountered and it may be a good idea to pack it in early.

Saturday, 27th

☽	#	♂	1:26
♂	⚼	♄	2:13
☽	⚻	♇	5:33
☽	□	♀	8:08
☽	→	♊	9:10
♀	→	♓	7:32PM
☽	△	☉	11:07
☽	⚻	♂	11:59

The high cautionary energy from yesterday will linger through today and should be handled carefully. Reread. Watch the early predawn for a period of aggressiveness and the late predawn for erratic irritability and coercive attitudes. The early to mid morning chips in with relationship issues. There will be a short Moon void of course period this morning from 8:08 to 9:10 when the Moon enters Gemini. At the point the energy will lift noticeably and general moods will tend to become more communicative. Moods will become more positive as the day wears on. Plan

January 2007   Pacific Time

☿	∥	♆	6:24
☽	□	♅	7:28
☽	☍	♃	8:46
☿	☍	♄	10:08
☿	#	♄	11:53
☽	△	♆	6:47PM

some sort of fun activity for the nighttime and know that very good moods should run through the late night and into tomorrow's predawn.

Sunday, 28th

Late Friday night social energy will run strongly into today's predawn, but you will want to watch for some minor erratic aggressiveness. There are three major energies running throughout the day. The first can bring about a certain spaciness, but is very positive for the intuitive process. Those involved in meditative processes should make the most of it. The second two combine into one and can be somewhat more cautionary. Watch for problems in communication and transportation, especially where limitations are encountered and resisted. On the other hand, this energy can be very good for negotiation and coming to long term agreement. This is an energy that should be handled carefully. Moods should mellow out through the nighttime. Relax and enjoy.

Monday, 29th

☽	✶	♄	1:05
☽	△	☿	3:16
☽	□	☉	3:51
☽	☍	♆	10:40
☽	—	♋	2:16PM
☿	∠	♂	3:15
☉	⚺	♂	3:37
☽	△	♀	6:41
☽	□	♆	9:45

High energy from yesterday may well linger through today and should be taken into account. There are two more major energies running throughout the day. The first can bring problems to communication and transportation, especially where people attempt to use force or impose their will on others. This may also result in an excess of thought and communication that can overload some people. The second is much more positive and can be used for any activity one may be involved in. Handling the cautionary energy well, this can be a go-for-it day. Good moods will run through the predawn and most of the morning. Watch the late morning for a period of coerciveness and be aware that the Moon will be void of course from 10:40 this morning until 2:16 this afternoon when it will enter Cancer. At that point the energy will lift noticeably and general moods will tend to become more sensitive and protective. Moods should be primarily positive following the void of course and through the evening. Choose well and enjoy.

Tuesday, 30th

☽	∠	♄	3:54
☽	☍	♂	8:46
☽	⚻	☉	9:09
☽	□	☿	10:04
☽	△	♅	1:31PM

Good moods should run through most of today's predawn. Watch the late predawn, however, for a brief period of hard attitudes. The late morning into the midday has scattered irritability with aggressiveness, erratic emotional reactions, and argumentativeness. Moods will improve through the

Astro-Weather

Pacific Time   January 2007

☽ ⚻ ♃ 3:20

afternoon, but be aware that the Moon will be void of course from 1:31 this afternoon through almost all of tomorrow. Relax and take it easy tonight.

Wednesday, 31ˢᵗ

☽ □ ♀ 12:52
☽ ⚻ ♆ 1:11
☽ ⚺ ♄ 7:14
☽ □ ♅ 5:17PM
☽ ⚻ ☿ 5:30
☽ ⚻ ♇ 5:37
☿ ⚹ ♆ 6:32
☽ □ ♃ 7:25
☽ — ♌ 9:15
☽ # ♂ 10:35

Yesterday's Moon void of course period runs right on through the daytime and finally ends at 9:15 tonight when the Moon enters Leo. At that point the energy will lift very noticeably and general moods will tend to become more intense and concerned with self, and tomorrow's full Moon will kick in. Try to lay low and tend to old business today. There is a major energy that is very good for seeing beneath the surface and coming to deeper understanding. Avoid making major changes based on these insights until after the void of course ends. Moods should be more positive than otherwise through the day, especially for those of us aware of and not fighting the void of course. Watch for minor irritabilities through the late afternoon to early evening.

Astro-Weather

February 2007

Overview

As February begins, Saturn continues to retrograde back from the trine to Pluto that lightened things up in recent months and toward an opposition to Neptune. This energy supports the illusions that various types of hardliners labor under and they will ignore the writing on the wall and continue to make trouble. This will become more intense as the month progresses and peak late this month and early next. Add to this the Jupiter square Uranus, which peaked late last month but remains through most of this month, and the headlines may well be spectacular. There will likely be flare-ups in any one or more of the various places where the current international conflict simmers, as well as in the U.S. culture war. The good news is that by the end of the month, Jupiter will begin to outrun Uranus and move toward a trine to Saturn and sextile to Neptune. This will frustrate hardliners as plans fail and support wanes. Fortunately, this aspect will tend to remain through early May. Jupiter, Saturn, Uranus and Neptune start to move into a more complicated configuration next month. All of this adds up to fits and starts for both those who seek to prolong the troubles and those seeking peace. Join in whatever global prayer and meditation efforts you become aware of.

On the more personal level, a very high energy full Moon is exact late on the 1st. This is part of a string of high positive energy days that run through the 4th or 5th. There are two particular periods to be careful in relationships. These are the 13th and 14th and again 23rd through 25th. You will also want to be aware of the Mercury retrograde period starting on the 13th and running through the 7th of next month. There are many more major energies, both positive and cautionary, to read ahead and be prepared for. The two most significant daytime Moon void of course periods are on the 10th and the 27th–28th.

Thursday, 1st

♄	#	♆	7:06
☽	⚻	♀	7:47
☽	#	♃	9:43
☽	⚻	♂	7:58PM
☉	⚺	♅	8:33
☽	⚻	♅	9:40
☽	☍	☉	9:46
☽	⚼	♇	9:57

Yesterday's positive energy will tend to linger through today, and now you can make good use of it. There are four other major energies running throughout today. The first is a long range outer planet aspect that emboldens hardliners in the international conflict. The second is very positive for any sort of technological endeavors and on higher octaves, magical technique and discipline. You will notice energy levels rising throughout the day as the full Moon takes

Pacific Time   February 2007

shape. It is exact at 9:46 tonight. Full Moons are always high energy and deserve to be approached with respect. The third easily leads to the exposure of things normally kept secret and hidden. This can come about unexpectedly. This energy can also bring problems with and for authority. The fourth indicates a general shift in thinking and communication patterns towards a more intuitive mode.

Friday, 2nd

☽ △ ♃	12:06
☉ ∠ ♇	12:15
☿ – ♓	1:22
☽ ☍ ♇	9:47
☽ # ☉	12:24PM
☽ # ♇	1:21
☽ ☌ ♄	3:33
☽ ∥ ♄	7:12
☽ # ♆	7:29

Consider the full Moon to run very strongly through today and much of tomorrow at least. There is another major energy coming into focus throughout the day that is very positive for any activity one may be involved in. This is excellent energy for technological and magical pursuits, but is also very amenable to the fun and stimulating. You may want to plan some sort of unusual social activity. Keep an eye on lingering energy from yesterday involving the exposure of secrets and problems with and for authority which will also run very strongly through today and into tomorrow. There will be an overriding sense of positivity, however, that will run through the day and peak tomorrow. Moods should be much more positive than otherwise, so make good choices and have a great time.

Saturday, 3rd

☽ ⊓ ♂	2:40
♂ ⚹ ♅	2:41
☽ △ ♇	2:54
☉ ∥ ♇	4:27
☽ – ♍	6:34
☉ ⚹ ♃	7:48
☽ ☍ ☿	10:26
☽ # ☿	3:01PM
☽ # ♀	8:35

High positive energy mentioned yesterday will run strongly through today. Plan all kinds of fun and stimulating activities. The full Moon energy is still hanging around and the most positive aspect connected to it peaks this morning. There is a Moon void of course period this morning running from 2:54 until 6:34 when the Moon enters Virgo. At that point the energy will lift and general moods will tend to become more discerning and concerned with detail. Moods will be positive through the void of course, but watch the late morning for minor argumentativeness. The mid afternoon may have another brief period of the same, and there will be minor relationship issues in the later evening. Don't let the little things mess up the fun.

Sunday, 4th

☽ ☍ ♀	12:09
☽ # ♅	6:32
☽ ☍ ♅	8:19
☽ △ ♂	10:07
☽ □ ♃	11:23
☽ ⚻ ☉	1:31PM

High energy from the past few days will tend to linger through today. Make good use of it and have fun. Watch the very early predawn for potential minor relationship issues. There may be erratic emotional reactions through the early morning, but good moods should run through the late morning. Take an active and fun approach. There may be minor

Astro-Weather

February 2007   Pacific Time

☾ ⚻ ♆   8:52

irritability in the early afternoon, but this should pass quickly. The rest of the afternoon through early evening is open, but watch the later evening for minor erratic spaciness which likely will pass unnoticed.

Monday, 5th

☾ ⚺ ♄   2:18
♂ ⚺ ♃   11:29
☾ □ ♇   2:36PM
☾ - ♎   6:15
☾ ⚼ ☉   10:27

There is a major energy running throughout today that is very positive for any activity one may be involved in. This is a go-for-it day. Get anything important done, however, before 2:36 this afternoon as the Moon will be void of course from then until 6:15 this evening when it enters Libra. At that point the energy will lift and general moods will tend to become more concerned with balance and beauty.

Tuesday, 6th

☾ ⚼ ♆   3:11
☾ ⚻ ☿   5:25
☾ ∠ ♄   8:22
☾ ⚻ ♀   7:27PM
☾ ∥ ♅   8:33
☾ ⚻ ♅   9:01
☉ # ♄   9:05

There is a major energy running throughout today that should be handled with care. It can bring about problems where people run into restriction and frustration, and have difficulty not acting out on it. It also easily brings trouble with and for authority. This is not the day to smart off to the boss or the traffic cop. Those who run afoul of this energy may well experience harsher and longer lasting consequences than usual. On the other hand, with self-discipline, much may be accomplished. Go for it, but carefully. There is scattered minor irritability from the mid predawn to the mid morning. The late morning through the afternoon opens up. But watch the evening to the late night for relationship issues and erratic emotional responses.

Wednesday, 7th

☾ ∥ ♀   12:11
☾ ⚹ ♃   12:41
☾ ∥ ☿   2:28
☾ □ ♂   2:41
☾ △ ☉   7:45
☾ △ ♆   9:45
♀ ☌ ♅   10:57
☾ ⚹ ♄   2:39PM
☉ ∥ ♆   2:46
☾ ⚼ ☿   2:54

Continue to deal carefully with the lingering energy from yesterday. There are two more major energies running through today. The first is highly social but erratic. It may be possible to make new starts in relationships, especially employing some unusual tactic. Surprise! On the other hand, you will want to be careful not to come off too crazy. The second can also go either way. This energy is very positive for meditative practices and the intuitive process, but it also tends to bring out the space cases. Watch for the alcohol and recreational drug-impaired as well as the otherwise out of it. If you meet someone who appears off their meds, they quite likely are. Minor aspects are mixed from the predawn through the mid afternoon, but are more positive than otherwise. Good moods should be especially dominant through the early and mid morning. Make good

Astro-Weather

choices with this day.

Thursday, 8th

☽	⚹	♇	3:38
☽	⚼	♅	3:39
☽	⚼	♀	5:31
☽	–	♏	7:09
☽	∠	♃	7:34
☽	//	☉	7:45
☉	☌	♆	7:53
☽	//	♆	8:49
☽	#	♄	10:12
☽	//	♇	3:27PM
♀	//	♅	6:14
☽	△	☿	11:45

The Moon will be void of course this morning from 3:38 until 7:09 when it enters Scorpio. At that point the energy will lift noticeably and general moods will tend to become more intense. There are three major energies running through the day. The first continues and intensifies yesterday's major energy for meditative practices, but also confusion and spaciness. The second continues the energy for new beginnings in relationships. Plan something fun, unusual, and stimulating, but don't get too carried away. That will be a tall order, however, as the third major aspect is excess party energy, pure and simple. This will be a very high energy day, but many will find it difficult to concentrate on work related matters. Watch for the partyhards who will be proving to themselves yet again that it is possible to get too much of a good thing. Minor aspects are mixed at best and good choices will be in order.

Friday, 9th

♀	□	♃	3:31
☽	∠	♇	9:57
☽	△	♅	10:02
☿	//	♅	1:41PM
☽	⚺	♃	2:09
☽	△	♀	3:14
☽	⚹	♂	7:21
☽	//	♃	9:29
☽	□	♆	10:26

The high social energy mentioned yesterday will remain very much with us through today and this may not be the most productive work day in the history of Fridays. There is another major energy running through the day that is very positive for initiating projects involving communication and transportation, as well as electricity, electronic media, technology, and magic. Moods should be positive through the predawn and early morning. The mid to late morning will be mixed. Avoid coercive attitudes and take a fun and innovative approach instead. Moods will be much more positive through the afternoon and early evening, but watch the late night for a downturn and a nosedive into tomorrow's predawn.

Saturday, 10th

☽	□	☉	1:50
☽	□	♄	2:38
☽	//	♂	3:38
☉	☍	♄	10:43
☽	⚺	♇	3:44PM
☽	–	♐	7:00

The high social energy from the past two days will attempt to run into today, to no avail. Today's predawn will turn sharply south and rotten moods will run rampant. Late Friday night party people be warned. There is a major energy running throughout the day that is significantly cautionary. Watch for people running into restriction and frustration and not responding well. Some of this will be due to excesses indulged over the past few days. This energy also brings problems with and for authority. Many will hit the wall today. Don't be one of them, or the wall

February 2007   Pacific Time

either. Also be aware that the Moon will be void of course from 2:38 this morning until 7:00 this evening when it enters Sagittarius. At that point the energy will lift very noticeably and general moods will tend to become more expansive and open to a wide range of ideas. The heavy energy will remain, but moods will improve following the void of course, and, being careful, something of a Saturday night might be salvaged.

Sunday, 11th

☽ ∠ ♂		2:45
☽ □ ☿		1:52PM
☽ □ ⛢		8:55
♂ ⚼ ♆		11:36

The high cautionary energy from yesterday will remain with us through today. Reread and apply. There is a major energy coming into focus throughout today, however, that is much more positive and can be used for fun activities. Be careful, but try to have a good time. Choose well.

Monday, 12th

☽ ☌ ♃		1:14
☽ □ ♀		7:50
☽ ⚹ ♆		8:33
☽ ⚼ ♂		9:05
☽ △ ♄		11:58
♀ ⚼ ♆		3:30PM
☽ ⚹ ☉		4:30

The positive energy from yesterday will remain with us through today and is joined by two more major energies. The first is very good for enjoying relationships. It is also good for fellowship along spiritual lines. The second is excellent for coming to greater balance and appreciating relationships, especially the male-female variety. Today's predawn is open and positive, but watch the early to mid morning for potential relationship issues. Once past that, good moods will run throughout the rest of the day at least. The later evening into the late night is open and the right choices will keep the glow going.

Tuesday, 13th

☽ ☌ ♆		12:44
☽ → ♑		3:42
☽ ∠ ♆		12:12PM
♀ ⚹ ♂		2:47
☽ ⚻ ♄		3:15
☿ ℞		8:31
☽ ∠ ☉		9:58
☽ ⚹ ☿		10:06

The Moon will be void of course this morning from 12:44 until 3:42 when it will enter Capricorn. At that point the energy will lift and general moods will tend to become more practical and concerned with accomplishment. Positive energy from yesterday will remain with us through most of today. There are two more major energies, however, that contradict. The first is this year's first Mercury retrograde which will run until March 7th. During a Mercury retrograde all things having to do with communication and transportation are prone to snafu and break down. Plan extra time for everything: watch for all manner of misunderstandings; avoid the signing of contracts and legal documents; and don't open new businesses. See the Mercury Retrograde page at the beginning of this book for more on these periods. The second slams the door on the positive relationship energy and easily leads to problems, especially

Astro-Weather

where hard, cold attitudes are indulged. Watch for erratic, irrational and unreasonable demands for change. Minor aspects are of no help and good choices are needed.

♀	⚻	♄	12:16
☽	⚹	♅	4:06
♂	⚻	♄	5:48
☽	⚺	♃	8:27
☽	⚺	♆	2:52PM
☽	⚻	♄	5:35
☽	☌	♂	6:19
☽	⚹	♀	7:23

Wednesday, 14th

The cautionary energy mentioned yesterday will linger through today. Be careful with it. There is another major energy that is also cautionary, and this one is potentially dangerous. Watch for sudden and erratic outbursts as people run into restrictions and frustrations. In extreme circumstances, people may become violent. Also be careful where energy and power are in use as accidents are more likely than usual. Be very careful in all these instances as consequences can be much harsher and longer lasting than normal. Aside from the major energies moods, should be primarily positive. Don't be among those caught up in the troubles. Do be aware that the Moon will be void of course from 7:23 this evning through much of tomorrow morning.

☽	∠	☿	12:10
☽	⚺	☉	2:18
☽	⚺	♇	5:53
☽	∠	♅	6:16
☽	→	♒	8:33
☽	∠	♃	10:38
☽	//	♂	5:03PM
☽	//	♃	6:45
☽	∠	♀	11:24

Thursday, 15th

Last night's Moon void of course period runs through most of the early morning and finally ends at 8:33 when the Moon enters Aquarius. At that point the energy will lift very noticeably and general moods will tend to become more independent and free thinking. Moods should be more positive than otherwise through the void of course. Relax and take it easy, but be prepared to hit the ground running as it ends. Watch the late morning for a brief period of exaggerated emotional responses, but for those not caught up in yesterday's nonsense, this is likely to pass unnoticed. Most of the rest of the day is open. Take an active and expansive approach through the late afternoon, and watch the very late night for minor relationship issues.

☽	⚺	☿	1:07
☽	∠	♇	7:14
☽	⚺	♅	7:39
☽	⚹	♃	12:04PM
☽	☌	♆	5:47
☽	☍	♄	7:56
☽	//	♇	7:59
☽	#	♄	11:19
☽	⚺	♂	11:40

Friday, 16th

There are two major energies coming into focus today. The first, which peaks early tomorrow morning, is excellent for looking within, coming to greater self understanding, and achieving more balance. Light will be shed on things normally kept secret and hidden, but not in a difficult way. You will notice energy levels rising throughout the day as the second major energy, tomorrow morning's new Moon, rolls in. Consider the new Moon to start today and be good. Today's very early predawn may have minor relationship issues, but good moods should run through the rest of the predawn. The early morning is mixed. Take a fun and inno-

February 2007   Pacific Time

vative approach, avoiding coerciveness. The rest of the daytime should be positive. Evening into the nighttime energies are mixed and good choices are needed.

Saturday, 17th

☽	∥	♆	1:50
☽	⌅	♀	2:36
☉	✶	♇	5:04
☽	✶	♇	8:00
☽	☌	☉	8:13
☽	–	♓	10:29
☽	∥	☉	2:04PM
☿	⌅	♂	5:09

Today is new Moon day. It is exact at 8:13 this morning. Remember that what you start at new Moon brings results at the next full Moon. This particular new to full period is more positive than many others we have seen. Be open to innovation and technology, and pay attention to relationships. Yesterday's positive energy for seeing beneath the surface remains very much with us through the day. Make good use of it. There is another major energy, however, that is rather more cautionary. Watch for problems in communication and transportation, especially where people become frustrated and aggressive. Also watch for problems along these lines reemerging from the past. Be aware of a Moon void of course period this morning running from 8:13 until 10:29 when the Moon enters Pisces. At that point the energy will lift and general moods will tend to become more mellow if a bit spacy. Have fun tonight, but be mindful of the cautionary energy and the new Moon. Be good.

Sunday, 18th

☽	☌	☿	12:42
☽	⌅	♂	1:28
♂	∥	♃	6:36
☽	∥	♅	7:15
☽	☌	♅	8:57
☽	∥	☿	1:11PM
☽	□	♃	1:30
☉	–	♓	5:10
☽	⌅	♆	6:46
☽	⚻	♄	8:29

Consider the new Moon from yesterday to run very strongly through today at least. There are two more major energies. The first is very good for beginning any project involving the use of energy and power. The second is the Sun's entry into the mutable water sign Pisces early this evening when the final third of the winter season begins. During this time, you will want to dream your dreams and make your plans for the beginnings of major projects at the Vernal Equinox next month. The early predawn may have a brief period of irritability and aggressiveness. Take an innovative approach through the early and mid morning. There may be some exaggerated emotional responses in the early afternoon. Moods will improve through the afternoon, but watch for some potential minor erratic hard attitudes in the later evening.

Monday, 19th – Presidents' Day

☽	∥	♀	12:27
☽	✶	♂	3:02
☽	☌	♀	7:43
☽	□	♇	8:43
☽	–	♈	11:06

There is a major energy running throughout today that is definitely of the cautionary persuasion. This aspect tends to stimulate a heavy and potentially coercive sexuality. While this may be interesting and even fun for some, it can be quite unsettling and dangerous for others. As always with

☽	⚺	☉	12:24PM
☽	#	♀	12:59
☽	∠	♆	7:05
♀	□	♇	7:53
☽	⚼	♄	8:37
☽	⚺	☿	10:43

this energy, protect the vulnerable. Moods should be more positive than otherwise through the early to mid predawn. Take a cooperative approach through the early morning, but watch the mid morning for potential coerciveness. Be aware that the Moon will be void of course this morning from 8:43 until 11:06 when enters Aries. At that point the energy will lift and general moods will tend to become more assertive and aggressive. Moods should be positive through the mid-day following the void of course, but do watch for relationship issues, especially in light of the major energy. Watch for spaciness and hard attitudes in the later evening.

Tuesday, 20th

☽	#	☿	2:12
☽	#	♅	7:02
☽	⚺	♅	9:43
☽	△	♃	2:32PM
☽	∠	☉	2:33
☽	⚹	♆	7:33
☽	#	☉	8:16
☽	△	♄	8:55
☽	∠	☿	9:40

Today's predawn is mixed but with the right choices, good moods are certainly possible. Take a friendly and communicative approach. Be open to innovation and the uses of technology through the morning. An unusual approach may yield surprising results. The afternoon is mixed, again, but good choices will result in a great deal more being accomplished than otherwise. Be on the lookout for those being disagreeable for no particularly good reason. Moods will lift and be more positive through the evening and into the late night. Practice some self-discipline for best results. There is a major energy occurring in tomorrow's early predawn which indicates a shift in relationships and aesthetic pursuits toward a more assertive and aggressive mode.

Wednesday, 21st

♀	→	♈	12:21
☽	□	♂	6:29
☽	△	♇	9:42
☽	∠	♅	10:25
☽	→	♉	12:03PM
☽	#	♆	12:40
☽	⚺	♀	1:09
☽	⚼	♃	3:24
☽	//	♄	3:47
☽	⚹	☉	5:03
☽	#	♇	6:43
☽	⚹	☿	8:47
☽	⚼	♇	10:44

Aside from the shift in relationship and aesthetic energy mentioned yesterday, today's predawn is open. Watch the very early morning for a period of aggressive attitudes and easily incited conflict. Moods will improve through the mid morning and a cooperative approach is recommended. Be aware that the Moon will be void of course from 9:42 this morning through 12:03 this afternoon when it enters Taurus. At that point the energy will lift noticeably and general moods will tend to become more down to earth and concerned with enjoyment. Relax and take it easy through the void of course, and tend to old business. Moods will be mixed following the void of course. Watch for minor spaciness, but that is followed by more positive relationship energy. Be on the lookout for exaggerated emotional responses and hard attitudes in the mid afternoon, but this will give way to much more positive moods through the late afternoon to early evening. Avoid a tendency toward coercive attitudes in the mid to late evening, and choose instead

February 2007   Pacific Time

☽	⚹	♅	11:32
☽	∠	♀	4:35PM
☽	⊼	♃	4:44
☽	#	♂	5:18
☉	☌	☿	8:44
☽	#	♃	8:46
☽	□	♆	9:40
☽	□	♄	10:40

☽	△	♂	11:47
☽	⊼	♇	12:19PM
☽	–	♊	2:42
☿	⊼	♀	4:21
☽	□	☿	8:06
☽	⚹	♀	8:47
☿	//	♅	9:28
♂	⊼	♆	9:44
☽	□	☉	11:56

☽	⚼	♂	3:28PM
☽	□	♅	3:28
♂	∠	♅	3:42
☽	☍	♃	9:12

a more positive and communicative approach.

Thursday, 22nd
There is a major energy running throughout the day that can be positive for looking within and coming to greater self-understanding. Remember that Mercury is retrograde and watch for issues from the past to pop up. Aside from the major energy, the early predawn is mixed. Avoid coerciveness and take a fun and innovative approach instead. Most of the rest of the predawn is open, but watch the late predawn to early morning for relationship issues, erratic emotional responses, and aggression. The rest of the daytime is open. Watch the later evening for exaggerated emotional responses, spaciness, and hard attitudes.

Friday, 23rd
The Moon will be void of course today from 11:47 this morning until 2:42 this afternoon when it will enter Gemini. At that point the energy will lift noticeably and general moods will tend to become more communicative. There are three major energies running throughout the day. The first should be positive for communication in relationships. Remember that Mercury is retrograde, however, and watch for people from the past. The second would normally be positive for beginning projects involving electricity, electronic media, technology, and magic. Again, remember that Mercury is retrograde and deal with projects already started along these lines. The third is very good for using energy and power behind the scenes. This will be a good day for doing those things you may not want the whole world to know about. This energy is also positive for making changes of all kinds. Minor aspects are mixed, but more positive than otherwise. Have fun tonight, but watch for a serious downturn later and pack it in early.

Saturday, 24th
High energy from yesterday will tend to linger through today and is joined by two more major energies, both of the cautionary persuasion. The first is the more dangerous of the two, and it easily brings about sudden, irrational violence, freak accidents and electrical fires. Watch for crazies and generally don't mess with people. The second, which can easily aggravate the first, brings about spaciness in relationships, especially where alcohol and other recreational substances are involved. Minor aspects are no help at all, and this will be a Saturday to lay low. Plan

Pacific Time   February 2007

tonight carefully.

Sunday, 25th

☽ △ ♆	2:02
☽ ✶ ♄	2:39
♀ ∠ ♆	4:28
♀ □ ♄	10:36
☽ ☍ ♆	5:21PM
♂ — ♒	5:32
☽ — ♋	7:48
☽ ⊼ ♂	7:56
☽ △ ☿	9:26

The high cautionary energy from yesterday will remain very much with us through today. It is joined by two more major energies. The first is related to yesterday's relationship energy and serves to make any problems that do occur much harsher and longer lasting than usual. Guard against feelings of restriction and frustration, and the urge to act out on them. The second indicates a general shift in the uses of energy and power toward a more independent and free-thinking mode. Aside from the major energies, good moods should run through the predawn. Most of the daytime is open. Watch for minor coercive attitudes in the late afternoon and be aware that the Moon will be void of course from 5:21 this afternoon until 7:48 tonight when it will enter Cancer. At that point the energy will lift and general moods will tend to become more sensitive and protective. Moods will be mixed following the void of course; choose well.

Monday, 26th

☽ □ ♆	5:13
☽ ∠ ♄	5:36
☽ □ ♀	7:42
☿ ✶ ♂	7:58
☽ △ ☉	9:57
☿ — ♒	7:01PM
☽ △ ♅	10:04
☽ □ ☿	11:02

There are three major energies running through today. The first would normally be positive for any activity involving communication and transportation. Bear in mind that Mercury remains retrograde, and it will be a good idea to use this energy on projects already started. The second indicates a general shift in thinking and communication toward a more independent and free-thinking mode. The third is very good for introspection and coming to deeper self-understanding. Learn from the past. Most of today's predawn is open, but watch the late predawn through early morning for spaciness, hard attitudes, and relationship issues. The mid through late morning will be much more positive. The rest of the daytime through most of the nighttime is open. Be aware of a long Moon void of course period starting at 10:04 tonight and running all the way through tomorrow.

Tuesday, 27th

☉ ∥ ☿	3:35
☽ ⊼ ♃	4:17
☽ ⊼ ♆	9:03
☽ ⚻ ♄	9:13
☽ □ ☉	4:11PM

Today is entirely covered by a long Moon void of course period. This will be one of those days to lay low, take it easy, and tend to old business. The energy for introspection and coming to deeper self-understanding mentioned yesterday will remain very much with us through today. Again, learn from the past. Watch the late predawn for erratic emotional overreactions. This will pass quickly, however, and

Astro-Weather

February 2007 — Pacific Time

it's unlikely that many will get caught up in it. The mid morning is mixed. Watch for an erratic spaciness and choose a disciplined, communicative approach. Aside from a brief period of minor irritability in the late afternoon, the afternoon into the late night is open

Wednesday, 28th

☽	⚻	♇	1:01
☽	⚻	☿	1:17
☽	□	♅	2:19
☽	—	♌	3:29
♄	☍	♆	3:55
☿	⚹	♆	5:13
☽	☍	♂	7:11
☽	□	♃	8:48
☽	#	♃	2:16PM
☽	△	♀	10:03
☽	⚻	☉	11:13
☽	#	♂	11:40

The long Moon void of course period finally ends at 3:29 this morning when the Moon enters Leo. At that point for those up and about, the energy will lift very noticeably and general moods will tend to become more practical and concerned with self. There are two major energies running throughout today. The first is a long range outer planet aspect that energizes hardliners in the ongoing international conflict. Watch the news also for earthquake and tidal wave activity. The second is very good for seeing beneath the surface and coming to greater understanding. Things from the past, in some cases including the deeply buried past, will tend to reemerge. Keep the eyes and ears open as there will be much to learn.

Pacific Time

March 2007

Overview

March starts out with the Saturn opposed Neptune very tight. This energy by itself enflames the passions of those believing that God is on their side and justifies whatever actions are taken. This is not confined to any one religion or sect and you will see hardliners of all stripes pushing their agendas, some with very unpleasant intent. The outer planet mix grows more complicated this month, however, and holds surprises for all sides on all fronts. Jupiter is slowing down as it moves toward a retrograde period that starts next month. But it still has the speed to get out ahead of the square to Uranus that has ratcheted up the tension during the past two months, and move on to trine and sextile the Saturn opposed Neptune. This will tend to diffuse tension as it peaks, and leave people wondering in just what directions are things going as there will be many contradictory events. Saturn will retro back from the opposition as the month wears on, but the fade will be slight and when it turns direct next month, will begin to tighten back up. This month and next will be interesting, to say the least. It will remain vitally important to support the gains made and add your energy to whatever global prayer and meditation for peace events may take place.

On the more personal levels, perhaps the biggest news is that the Mercury retrograde period that started on February 13th will end on the 7th. See the Retrograde pages at the front of the book for more on these periods. As Mercury stations and turns direct through the first half of the month, it will spend many days in semi-sextile to Pluto. This will be a period of gaining access to information normally kept secret and hidden, as well as being unavailable for other reasons. Focus on learning from or about the past until the 7th or 8th and from the now through the 19th or so. There is very high social and relationship energy when the 7th–9th features a grand trine involving Venus, Jupiter and Saturn. The 21st through 23rd has high but contradictory Mars energy. There are many more high energy days to read ahead and plan for dealing with. The most significant daytime Moon void of course periods are on the 22nd and the 26th–27th.

Thursday, 1st

☽ ☌ ♆ 5:46
☽ ⚻ ⛢ 7:11

High energy from yesterday will remain very much with us through today. The headlines are likely blaring. There is an-

March 2007   Pacific Time

☽ △ ♃	1:54PM
♂ ∠ ♃	1:56
☽ ☌ ♄	6:12
☽ ☍ ♆	6:32
☽ # ♇	8:23
☽ ∥ ♄	10:40

other major energy running through the day that easily leads to over-expenditures of energy and power. Watch for some people to promise more than they can deliver, overreach themselves, and generally get too carried away. This is not a good energy in combination with the previous. Today's early predawn is mixed, but most of the rest of the predawn is open. Watch the late predawn through early morning for coercive attitudes, general unpleasantness, and erratic emotional responses. Moods will improve through the rest of the morning and be much more positive in the early to mid afternoon. Take a disciplined approach through the evening. Avoid spaciness and scratchy attitudes.

Friday, 2nd

☽ # ♆	3:57
☽ ⚻ ♀	6:23
☽ ☍ ☿	7:54
☽ △ ♇	11:03
☽ — ♍	1:32PM
☿ ∠ ♀	4:55
☽ ⚺ ♂	9:14

High energy from the past few days will remain strongly in effect and is joined by two more energies today. The first easily leads to problems in relationships as issues from the past resurface. Don't think it, and if you do think it, certainly don't say it. You will notice energy levels rising throughout the day as the second energy, tomorrow's full Moon, rolls in. Watch the mid predawn to the mid morning for spaciness, relationship issues, and argumentativeness. Moods will improve in the late morning, but be aware that the Moon will be void of course from 11:03 this morning until 1:32 this afternoon when it will enter Virgo. At that point the energy will lift and general moods will tend to become more discerning and concerned with detail. The rest of the afternoon through the early evening is open. Watch the later evening for minor irritability and aggressiveness. Have fun tonight, but remember the full Moon and be careful.

Saturday, 3rd

☽ # ☿	1:49
☉ ⚺ ♀	10:24
☉ ∥ ♅	10:45
☽ ☍ ☉	3:17PM
☽ ⚹ ☉	3:20
☽ ⚺ ♀	3:23
☽ # ♅	4:08
☽ # ☉	4:30
☽ ☍ ♅	6:28

Today is full Moon day. It is exact at 3:17 this afternoon. Remember that full Moons are always high energy and deserve to be approached with respect. This particular full Moon is more positive than many we have had and is an eclipse which serves to intensify its effects. There are two more major energies running throughout the day, both related to the full Moon. The first is positive for communication in relationships. Light will be shed. The second would normally be very good for beginning any project involving science, technology and magic. Mercury, however, is still retrograde and it will be a good idea to focus on projects already in the works. Aside from the major energies, there may be a brief period of irritability in the early to

Pacific Time March 2007

mid predawn, but this is likely to pass unnoticed. Most of the daytime is open, but watch the mid afternoon through the early evening for scattered minor irritability. Have fun later, but do be careful.

Sunday, 4th

☽	∥	♀	12:26
☽	□	♃	1:36
☽	⚻	♂	5:07
☽	⚺	♄	5:11
☽	⚻	♆	6:04
☽	⚻	☿	5:15PM
☽	□	♇	10:56
♀	⚺	♅	11:05

Consider the full Moon to run very strongly through today at least. There are two more major energies coming into focus. The first is positive for relationships. Plan some sort of fun, unusual and stimulating activity. The second is related to yesterday's energy for projects involving technology and magic. Those so inclined should make good use of it. There may be some exaggerated emotional reactions in the early predawn. The late predawn to early morning is mixed. Take a disciplined approach and avoid aggression and spaciness. Most of the rest of the daytime is open, but the late afternoon to early evening may have a period of erratic irritability, which will pass quickly. Watch for another downturn in the late night. Also be aware that the Moon will be void of course from 10:56 tonight into tomorrow's predawn.

Monday, 5th

☽	→	♎	1:25
☉	♂	♅	7:39
☽	⚹	♄	11:14
☽	⚻	♆	12:24PM
☽	△	♂	1:25
☽	#	♀	8:48
☽	∥	☉	9:09
☽	⚻	☿	10:53
☉	#	♀	11:12

Last night's Moon course period ends this morning at 1:25 when the Moon enters Libra. At that point the energy will lift and general moods will tend to become more concerned with balance and beauty. The energy mentioned over the past few days for beginning projects involving technology and magic peaks this morning and, again, those involved in these things should make the most of it. Remember that Mercury is retrograde, however, and focus on things already begun. There is another major energy coming into focus throughout the day that is positive for gaining insight into and understanding of relationships. Light will be shed and you will want to make good use of it. Aside from the major energies, the predawn following the void of course and most of the morning is open. Watch the late morning through midday for hard attitudes and spaciness. Take an active approach and get a lot done through the rest of the afternoon. There may be minor relationship issues in the late night.

Tuesday, 6th

☽	∥	♅	12:57
☽	⚻	♅	7:16
☽	⚻	☉	9:19

Lingering effects from the high energy of the past several days are likely to remain with us through today. Try to take a friendly yet innovative approach through the early pre-

Astro-Weather

March 2007   Pacific Time

☽	☍	♀	10:48
☽	⚹	♃	2:42PM
☽	⚹	♄	5:30
☽	△	♆	6:55
☽	∥	☿	9:23

dawn. The rest of the predawn to the very early morning is open. Watch rest of the morning for erratic emotional responses, irritability, and relationship issues. Once past that, moods will begin to become more positive. The mid afternoon has positive, good mood energy. A disciplined approach through the evening will yield very good results. People will tend to feel social and friendly through the evening. Make good choices and get the most from all of this.

Wednesday, 7th

☽	△	☿	5:00
☽	⚹	♇	11:51
☽	□	♅	1:53PM
☽	∥	♆	2:09
☽	–	♏	2:16
♀	#	♅	4:27
☽	□	☉	6:36
☽	#	♄	8:35
☿	D		8:45
☽	⚼	♃	9:23
☽	∥	♇	10:14

There are three major energies running through the day. The first is cautionary and can easily lead to problems in relationships. Watch for sudden unrealistic and irrational demands for change. With the best of choices, this energy can be positive, by focusing on fun, innovative, and unusual things. The second is Mercury turning direct late tonight after having backed up in our skies since February 13th. Over the next several days, as Mercury picks up speed, the unusually high number of problems involving communication and transportation that we have had over the past few weeks will fade. The third is high social energy, pure and simple. The only problem with this is that people have a tendency to get carried away. Be aware of a Moon void of course period from 11:51 this morning until 2:16 this afternoon when the Moon enters Scorpio. At that point the energy will lift noticeably and general moods will tend to become more intense. Minor aspects are mixed throughout the day, choose well.

Thursday, 8th

♀	△	♃	3:15
☽	□	♂	6:29
☽	∥	♂	12:28PM
☽	⚼	♆	6:15
☽	△	♅	8:23

The high social energy mentioned yesterday will remain very much with us through today and is joined by another major related energy. This aspect is excellent for strengthening and solidifying relationships. Make a positive gesture in an appropriate situation through this period and it is likely to be reciprocated. Problems can set in where attempts are made in inappropriate situations. There is another major energy that does easily lead to getting carried away, which will come into focus today and peak tomorrow. Handled properly, this period can be very positive, but have a sense of proportion. Minor aspects are mixed at best so choose very well.

Friday, 9th

| ♀ | △ | ♄ | 12:41 |

High positive energy for relationships continues very

Pacific Time   March 2007

☽ △ ☉	3:42
☽ ⚹ ♃	3:54
☽ □ ♄	5:52
☽ ∥ ♃	6:17
☉ □ ♃	6:18
☽ ⚻ ♀	6:30
☽ □ ♆	7:48
☽ □ ☿	5:51PM
♀ ⚹ ♆	7:41

strongly through today, but again, remember to keep things in perspective. It will be very easy for some people to get carried away, over-enthusiastic, and to shoot for stars that are out of reach. There are three additional major energies coming running throughout today. The first is the essence of excess. People will be tending to over-optimism, overindulgence, and over-doing. Realistic expectations may be easily and wonderfully reached. Ill-considered overreaching can lead to deep disappointment and harsh reactions. The second is more positive relationship energy that will mostly be used socially. The third is the hitting the wall, bottom line energy that will affect those who get caught up in the various manifestations of excess. Be aware that the Moon will be void of course from 5:51 this afternoon into tomorrow's predawn. This will be a very high energy, social Friday night. Have fun, but remember the cautions and the void of course.

Saturday, 10th

☽ ⚹ ♆	12:18
☽ – ♐	2:36
☉ ⚻ ♄	4:21
☽ ⚼ ♀	3:37PM
☽ ⚹ ♂	11:19

Last night's Moon void of course period runs through much of today's predawn and ends at 2:36 this morning when the Moon enters Sagittarius. At that point the energy will lift and general moods will tend to become more expansive and open to a wide range of ideas. There is another major energy coming into focus throughout the day that is highly social, but you will want to watch for spaciness and excessive partying. This can be in harsh contrast to those handling the high energy well. There are going to be those getting it and those not. Those not are not going to be happy about it. Have fun today and tonight, but watch for the grumpy.

Sunday, 11th – Daylight Savings Begins

☉ ⚹ ♆	7:30
☽ □ ♅	9:02
☽ ☌ ♃	4:20PM
☽ △ ♄	5:33
☽ ⚹ ♆	7:51
☽ □ ☉	8:52

The high energy from the past several days will remain with us through today, for good or ill. Hopefully you are among those who handled it correctly. Today's predawn starts out with positive moods and the rest of the predawn through early morning is open. Watch the mid morning for a period of irritability which may pass unnoticed, and may not. Take an expansive approach through the afternoon and into the early evening. Good moods should run through the early evening, but the later evening has the potential for a significant downturn with a period of what may become really rotten moods. Choices.

Astro-Weather

March 2007   Pacific Time

☽ △ ♀	12:45
☽ ⚺ ♂	6:02
☽ ✶ ☿	6:41
☽ ☌ ♇	11:25
☽ — ♑	1:33PM
☽ ⚃ ♄	9:43

Monday, 12th
Today's predawn starts out with good moods and most of the rest of the predawn is open. The late predawn to early morning is mixed. Watch for aggressiveness and choose a friendly and communicative approach instead. Be aware that the Moon will be void of course from 11:25 this morning until 1:33 this afternoon when it enters Capricorn. At that point the energy will lift and general moods will tend to become more practical and concerned with accomplishment. The rest of the afternoon following the void of course and on through the evening is open. Watch the later evening for some potential hard attitudes.

☽ ⚺ ♆	12:09
☽ ⚺ ☿	11:34
☽ ⚼ ♂	11:37
☽ ✶ ♅	5:29PM

Tuesday, 13th
Watch today's very early predawn for a brief period of spaciness. The rest of the predawn through the mid morning is open. The late morning to midday is mixed. Watch for minor irritability and argumentativeness. Choose a communicative, active and friendly approach instead. The rest of the afternoon is open and good moods should run through the late afternoon early evening. The rest of the evening into the late night is open to positive.

☽ ⚼ ♃	12:21
☽ ⚻ ♄	12:56
☽ ⚼ ♆	3:29
☽ ✶ ☉	8:43
☽ □ ♀	1:19PM
☽ ⚼ ☿	3:34
☽ ⚼ ♇	5:54
☽ — ♒	7:50
☽ ⚺ ♅	8:14

Wednesday, 14th
Today's early predawn is mixed. Take a communicative and expansive approach and avoid feelings of restriction and frustration. The mid predawn comes back more social and positive. Good moods should run through the rest of the morning to midday. Watch the early afternoon for relationship issues. Get anything important done before 1:19 this afternoon as the Moon will be void of course from then until 7:50 tonight when it enters Aquarius. At that point the energy will lift noticeably and general moods will tend to become more independent and free-thinking. Watch for a period of erratic irritability following the void of course, but this will pass quickly.

☽ ⚺ ♃	2:53
☽ ∥ ♃	5:12
☽ ⚺ ☉	12:49PM
☽ ☌ ♂	7:24
☽ ⚺ ♇	7:42
☽ ⚼ ♅	10:02

Thursday, 15th
There will be a major energy coming into focus throughout today that is highly cautionary. Watch for secret and coercive activities up to and including violence. Under no circumstances allow yourself to be drawn into altercations with strangers. Aside from the major energy, go for it through the morning, taking an expansive approach. There may be some minor irritability through the midday, but this should pass unnoticed by most of us. Take an active ap-

proach through the evening, but remember the cautionary energy and be much more careful than usual.

♂	∠	♇	1:13
☽	∥	♂	3:05
☽	⚹	♃	4:30
☽	☍	♄	4:36
☽	☌	♆	7:17
☽	∥	♇	8:09
☽	#	♄	8:44
☽	∥	♆	3:02PM
♃	△	♄	3:42
☽	⚺	☉	3:52
☿	⚹	♇	4:33
♀	△	♇	5:17
☿	⚹	♀	6:25
☽	⚹	♇	8:41
☽	☌	☿	8:54
☽	⚹	♀	8:59
☽	—	♓	10:29

Friday, 16th

Yesterday's highly cautionary energy will remain with us through today. Reread and apply. It is joined by four more major energies. The first is a long-range outer planet aspect that is positive and there will be some indications of progress being made in the ongoing international conflict. There are other energies at work in this arena, however, and we are far from finished with this round of nonsense. The second is very good for seeing beneath the surface and coming to greater understanding. Things that are normally kept secret and hidden will be more accessible and positive changes can be made. The third is very good for taking relationships to deeper levels. There may be a heavier sexual component to this than some people are comfortable with, so be more sensitive in situations requiring it. The fourth is very positive for communication in relationships. This is in good combination with the previous energy. Make a positive gesture in an appropriate situation and it may well be reciprocated. Remember to try not to move things along too fast unless you are certain. Minor aspects are mixed throughout the day but good choices should yield good moods and a fun time. Be aware that the Moon will be void of course tonight from 8:59 until 10:29 when it enters Pisces. The energy will then lift and general moods will tend to become more mellow if a bit spacy. Avoid new things during the void of course.

☽	∥	☿	1:15
☽	#	♀	4:07
♀	—	♉	3:00PM
☽	∥	♅	9:18
♀	∠	♅	10:56
☽	⚺	♂	11:22
☽	☌	♅	11:25
☽	∠	♀	11:28

Saturday, 17th

High energy from yesterday will run strongly through today. Make good choices and keep the positive glow going. There are three more major energies running through today. The first is cautionary relationship energy. Watch for sudden unrealistic and unreasonable demands for change. This will most likely affect those who pushed too far or too hard yesterday. The second is much more positive and is excellent for any sort of fun, unusual and stimulating activities one may be involved in. On higher octaves this energy is great for magical technique and discipline. You will notice energy levels rising throughout the day as tomorrow's New Moon comes into focus.

♂	⚺	♅	12:25

Sunday, 18th

Today is new Moon day. It is exact at 7:42 tonight. Re-

☿	→	♓	2:32
☽	⚻	♄	5:18
☽	□	♃	5:35
☽	⚺	♆	8:10
☿	#	♀	11:10
☽	//	☉	4:11PM
☉	●	☽	7:32
☽	☌	☉	7:42
☽	□	♇	8:58
☽	#	☉	9:14
☽	→	♈	10:41
☽	⚺	☿	11:52

member that what you start at new Moon tends to bring results at the next full Moon. During this new to full period it will be a very good idea to focus on self-discipline issues. This new Moon is also an eclipse, which serves to intensify everything connected to it. The cautionary relationship energy mentioned yesterday will remain with us through today. If trouble pops up, switch to damage control. The energy for fun and stimulating activities will also remain with us through today. There is another energy that can be very good for communication in relationships. There may be a certain compulsiveness to it that can aggravate the cautionary relationship energy mentioned above. Late Saturday night social scenes are likely to be highly energized well into today's predawn. Have fun but remember the relationship minefield and step lightly. Also remember the new Moon and be good along all lines. Minor aspects are mixed at best through the predawn and morning period. Watch the later evening for a coercive irritability and be aware that the Moon will be void of course tonight from 8:58 until 10:41 when it will enter Aries. At that point the energy will lift and general moods will tend to become more assertive and aggressive.

Monday, 19th

☽	∠	♂	12:32
☽	⚺	♀	1:26
☽	⚼	♄	5:03
☽	∠	♆	8:01
☉	□	♇	3:13PM
☽	#	♅	4:06
☽	⚺	♅	11:14

Consider the new Moon to remain very much with us through today and well into tomorrow. There is another major energy running through today that is definitely of a cautionary nature. Watch for secret and coercive activities of all kinds. Light will be shed on these sorts of things, in unexpected ways. Guard your secrets and keep the eyes and ears open as there will be much to learn. This energy also brings problems with and for authority. Watch the headlines for leadership changes and do not mess with the boss or other authority figures. Minor aspects are of very little to no help, and this will be a day for making very good choices.

Tuesday, 20th

☽	∠	☿	1:05
☽	⚹	♂	1:32
☽	△	♄	4:42
☽	△	♃	5:19
☽	⚹	♆	7:49
☽	#	☿	10:15
☽	//	♀	2:59PM
☉	→	♈	5:07
☽	△	♇	8:33

High energy from the past few days is likely to spill over into today. Reread the cautions and apply them. The Sun enters the cardinal fire sign Aries at 5:07 this afternoon and the spring season begins. This is the Vernal Equinox and is the time to initiate major projects for this solar cycle. Just as the farmer plants in the spring to harvest in the fall, we can sow the seeds of what we wish to harvest. Today is among the most important days of the year. For those not caught up in lingering unpleasantness from the past few days, this

Pacific Time   March 2007

☽	#	♆	9:45
☽	–	♉	10:15
☽	⚼	☉	10:37
☽	∠	♅	11:10

should be a much better day. Good moods will run strongly from the early predawn through much of the morning. The afternoon is mostly open, but pay some positive attention to important relationships. Good moods should continue during the evening and into the late night, but be aware that the Moon will be void of course tonight from 8:33 until 10:15 when it will enter Taurus. At that point the energy will lift and general moods will tend to become more down to earth and concerned with enjoyment.

Wednesday, 21st

☽	⚹	☿	2:32
☽	∥	♄	4:13
☽	#	♇	4:25
☽	#	♂	4:49
☽	☌	♀	5:11
☽	⚏	♃	5:18
♀	⚏	♃	6:40
♂	∥	♆	3:58PM
♂	#	♄	8:31
☽	⚏	♆	8:41
☽	⚹	♅	11:26

High energy continues through today with the addition of three more major energies. The first is highly social but easily leads to overindulgence. Watch for people proving to themselves yet again that it is possible to get too much of a good thing. The second is very good for initiating deep changes in the way one uses energy and power. It is possible to put very interesting projects into motion, but keep an eye on motives. Yours and others. The third is connected to the second and needs to be handled carefully. Positive use will involve greater self-discipline. Watch for any tendency, however, to run up against restrictions and frustrations and to act out on them. This will be a day to make very good use of, but it needs to be dealt with in a very conscious and positive way. Aside from the major energies, minor aspects are mixed in the predawn. The rest of the day through the evening is open, but watch for some minor coercive irritability in the later evening.

Thursday, 22nd

☽	∠	☉	12:32
☽	□	♂	4:15
☽	□	♄	4:42
☽	⚻	♃	5:40
☽	#	♃	6:41
☽	□	♆	8:12
♂	☍	♄	12:33PM
☽	⚻	♇	9:22
☽	–	♊	11:07

There is a major energy running throughout today that is very related to yesterday's. You will want to be even more on guard against feelings of restriction and frustration. Those who compulsively react to these things may very well end up with much harsher and longer-lasting consequences than usual. A positive and expansive approach will yield much better results, and thankfully there is a related major energy coming into focus that does lead in that direction. Choices will be very important today. Minor aspects through the predawn and early morning will be of no help. What may be a blessing in disguise and which may help to blunt the effects of the cautionary energy is that the Moon will be void of course from 8:12 this morning until 11:07 tonight when it will enters Gemini. At that point the energy will lift noticeably and general moods will tend to become more communicative.

March 2007   Pacific Time

☽	⚹	☉	3:08
☽	□	☿	7:22
♂	⚹	♃	9:00
☽	⩟	♀	10:56

Friday, 23rd

There is a major energy running throughout today that is related to the energies from the past several days. Fortunately, this energy caps it all off with positivity. Take an expansive approach. Those who have been having problems may be able to sort them out and those who have been using the energy well should be able to make significant progress. Good moods will run through the predawn. Watch the early morning for a brief period of irritability and argumentativeness. This will pass quickly and good moods should run through the rest of the day and into the late night.

☽	□	♅	1:49
☽	⚹	♄	7:03
☽	☍	♃	8:24
☽	△	♂	9:43
♄	#	♇	10:54
☽	△	♆	11:03
☉	⚼	♄	11:57
♀	#	♆	12:58PM
☽	⩘	♀	3:13

Saturday, 24th

High energy just continues to roll, with three major energies running through today. The first is a long range outer planet energy that harkens all the way back to 9/11. There will be efforts by hardliners to make sure the world knows that this is not over. Watch the news ... or don't, as you are so inclined. The second easily leads to problems with authority, older people, and traditional matters. Watch for people creating trouble for themselves, getting into disputes they cannot win. This energy also brings trouble to those in leadership positions. The third, cautionary as well, easily leads to confusion and spaciness in relationships, especially where recreational substances and the otherwise out of it are involved. Minor aspects are once again mixed and good choices will be needed. This will be a high energy Saturday night, but one to be very careful with.

☽	☍	♆	12:58
☽	—	♋	2:49
☽	⩘	♄	9:29
♂	☌	♆	10:38
☽	□	☉	11:17
☽	⚼	♆	1:45PM
☽	⚼	♂	1:56
☽	△	☿	4:24
☽	⚹	♀	8:42

Sunday, 25th

The Moon will be void of course this morning from 12:58 until 2:49 when it will enter Cancer. At that point the energy will lift and general moods will tend to become more sensitive and protective. There are two major energies running through today. The first needs to be handled carefully. On higher octaves, it is positive for making new beginnings along spiritual lines. On lower octaves you will want to watch out for spaciness and confusion, especially around the beginnings of projects. Also keep an eye out for the space cases, who are likely to be on parade. The second highlights relationship issues, for good or ill. Watch the mid morning through the mid afternoon for hard attitudes, rotten moods, spaciness, and potential minor aggression. Take a long walk by yourself. From the late afternoon on, moods will lighten significantly, and most of us will become fit for human interaction once again.

Pacific Time   March 2007

♀	#	♂	4:18
☽	△	♅	7:36
☽	⌣	♄	12:48PM
☽	⚻	♃	2:33
☽	⚻	♆	5:21
☽	⚻	♂	7:14
☉	∠	♆	9:20
☽	⚼	☿	10:52

Monday, 26th
Relationship energy from yesterday will continue through today. Deal carefully with significant others. There is another major energy that is cautionary to say the least. Watch for all manner of spaciness and confusion. Those overindulging alcohol and other recreational substances will be out and about. Many will be those who seem to have slipped off their meds. The predawn is open. Good moods should run through the morning and midday. The Moon will be void of course, however, from 7:36 this morning through tomorrow morning. Relax and take it easy through today and tend to old business.

☽	⚻	♆	8:06
☽	-	♌	10:05
☽	⚼	♅	11:51
☽	⚼	♃	6:57PM
☽	#	♃	7:53
☽	△	☉	11:53

Tuesday, 27th
Yesterday's long Moon void of course period runs through the most of the morning and finally ends at 10:05 this afternoon when the Moon enters Leo. At that point the energy will lift very noticeably and general moods will tend to become more intense and concerned with self. Watch the midday following the void of course for a brief period of erratic irritability. This will pass quickly and probably won't even be noticed by most of us. Take an expansive approach through the evening, but watch for some tendency toward exaggerated emotional responses. Moods will improve markedly in the very late night.

☽	⚻	☿	6:32
☽	□	♀	11:06
☽	⚼	♇	12:56PM
♀	#	♇	3:29
☽	⚻	♅	4:52
♀	∥	♄	7:10
☽	☌	♄	9:55

Wednesday, 28th
There are three major energies running through today, all of them at least somewhat cautionary. The first easily leads to a heavy and potentially coercive sexuality. While this can be fun for some, it can be unsettling and even dangerous for others. Protect the vulnerable. The second can be positive for strengthening and solidifying relationships. On the other hand, some may feel restriction and frustration, which is in bad combination with the first. The third, unfortunately, is a reprise and strengthening of the first. This really is a day to be very careful in your dealings with all others, especially those in potentially intimate situations. Today's predawn will start out with very positive moods. Minor aspects are primarily irritable through most of the daytime, however, and good choices will be necessary.

☽	△	♃	12:06
☽	∥	♀	2:27
☽	☍	♆	3:03

Thursday, 29th
The high cautionary relationship energy from the past two days will remain with us through today. Reread and apply carefully. There is another major energy running through

Astro-Weather

March 2007   Pacific Time

☽	∥	♄	3:04
☽	#	♇	3:24
♀	⚻	♇	5:57
♂	∥	♆	6:52
☽	⚻	☉	7:39
☽	☍	♂	8:45
☽	#	♆	11:58
☽	#	♂	12:13PM
☽	△	⚷	6:23
☽	–	♍	8:27

the day that is a continuation of energy from the 25th. This needs to be handled carefully. On higher octaves, it can be positive for making new beginnings along spiritual lines. But on lower octaves you will want to watch out for spaciness and confusion, especially around the beginnings of projects. The early predawn starts out with good moods, but watch the mid predawn for relationship issues, spaciness, hard attitudes, and coercion. The early through mid morning chips in with general irritability and aggression. The midday contributes spaciness and more aggressiveness. Moods will improve through the rest of the afternoon and into the evening. Be aware that the Moon will be void of course this evening from 6:23 until 8:27 when it will enter Virgo. At that point the energy will lift and general moods will tend to become more discerning and concerned with detail.

Friday, 30th

| ☽ | ⊼ | ☉ | 4:07PM |
| ☽ | # | ☿ | 4:18 |

There is a major energy coming into focus throughout the day that is highly social and fun-oriented, and after the past several days we have it coming. Plan some sort of unusual and stimulating activities with those close to you, and have a great time.

Saturday, 31st

☽	☍	☿	12:55
♀	⚹	⚳	1:21
☽	#	⚳	1:46
☽	☍	⚳	4:42
☽	△	♀	5:03
☽	⚺	♄	9:27
☽	∥	☉	10:05
☽	□	♃	11:58
☽	⊼	♆	3:02PM
♇	℞		3:46
☉	⚼	♂	4:21

The high fun and social energy mentioned yesterday will remain with us through today. Choose to focus on it. There is another major energy that is rather more cautionary. Watch for some people to be easily aggravated, which in extreme cases can lead to violence. This energy can bring problems with and for authority, and there may be attempts at regime change on many levels. Light will be shed on the uses of energy and power, and this aspect is likely to lead to some headlines. Minor aspects are mixed through most of the predawn, but good moods should run from the late predawn through much of the morning. The late morning through the nighttime is mixed at best. Choices.

April 2007

Overview

As April begins, the Saturn opposed Neptune is weaker but still well within orb, and Jupiter is tightly in trine to Saturn and sextile Neptune. This complex will hold throughout the month and Uranus will move more tightly into it to complicate things even further. By the end of the month, Uranus will be in square to Jupiter, quincunx to Saturn, and semi-sextile to Neptune. It is impossible to predict with any accuracy just how all of this energy will play out in the international conflict and in the US culture war, but it is certain to be interesting. What most likely will occur is a great deal of activity in all theatres, but with much contradiction. Things will seem to be getting better one minute and doom will loom the next. And this will all vary according to viewpoint. It is likely, however, that things will turn out better than worse, and it all may amount to a great deal more noise than action. Of course, that will be of little consolation if you or a loved one is where something really does happen. I will say that Jupiter's involvement greatly increases the probability that whatever happens will seem worse than it really is, and will have much in the way of silver linings. Support the peace initiatives and make the most of the positives in this confusing configuration.

On the more personal level, you will want to be careful in relationships and social situations around the full Moon on the 2nd. There is a very positive period running from the 7th through the 9th. This is a grand trine involving the Sun, Jupiter and Saturn. Mercury forms the same angles from the 20th through 21st. Be sure to make good use of both of these periods. There are many more high energies, both positive and otherwise, to read ahead and make plans for dealing with. The most significant daytime Moon void of course period is on the 23rd.

Sunday, 1st

☽	⚻	♂	12:54
☽	□	♇	6:37
☽	→	♎	8:43
☿	☌	♅	11:28
☽	⚼	♀	2:45PM
☽	∠	♄	3:42
☽	⚼	♆	9:28

The Moon will be void of course this morning from 6:37 until 8:43 when it will enter Libra. At that point the energy will lift and general moods will tend to become more concerned with balance and beauty. There are three major energies running throughout today. The first is very good for beginning projects involving communication, transportation, electricity, technology, and on higher octaves, magic. The second easily brings problems to relationships. Guard

April 2007   Pacific Time

against feelings of restriction and frustration, and acting out on them. Problems in this area that are indulged today can lead to more severe and longer-lasting consequences than usual. You will notice energy levels rising throughout the day as tomorrow's full Moon rolls in. Minor aspects are no help, and this is a day for good choices.

Monday, 2nd

♀	□	♄	12:00
☽	#	☉	12:16
☽	//	♅	5:51
☽	⚻	♂	9:25
☽	//	☿	10:02
☽	☍	☉	10:15
☽	⚹	♅	5:43PM
☽	⚹	☿	9:37
☽	✶	♄	10:04

Today is full Moon day. It is exact at 10:15 this morning. Remember that full Moons are always high energy and deserve to be approached with caution. With this particular full Moon, you will want to concentrate on self-discipline. The cautionary relationship energy mentioned yesterday will tend to linger through today and there are two more major energies coming into focus. The first easily leads to problems in communication and transportation, especially where people run into restrictions and frustrations that pop up unexpectedly and out of nowhere. The third is high but erratic social energy that can easily run out of control. Minor aspects are little to no help and this is definitely a day for good choices.

Tuesday, 3rd

☽	⚹	♀	12:35
☽	✶	♃	12:50
☿	⚹	♄	1:18
♀	⚹	♃	2:59
☽	△	♆	4:00
☽	//	♂	2:14PM
☽	△	♂	5:58
☽	✶	♇	7:29
☽	//	♆	8:25
☽	–	♏	9:35

Consider the full Moon to run through today and well into tomorrow. Yesterday's cautionary energies will remain with us through today as well. Continue to be careful in all your dealings with others, especially in situations involving communication and transportation. Also continue to be on the lookout for people getting carried away with the social energy. Many will find it hard to focus on work. There is another major energy coming into focus throughout the day that also easily brings problems to communication and transportation. Difficulties will arise where people attempt to say and do too much. Don't bite off more than you can chew and don't make promises you're not sure you can deliver on. Minor aspects are mixed, but good moods are available to those making the right choices. Be aware that the Moon will be void of course tonight from 7:29 until 9:35 when it will enter Scorpio. At that point the energy will lift and general moods will tend to become more intense.

Wednesday, 4th

☿	□	♃	12:16
☽	⚻	♅	12:17
☽	//	♆	5:24

High energy continues through today. Full Moon and the cautionary energy from the past couple days will linger and are joined by five more major energies. The first can be

☽ # ♄ 6:07
☽ ∠ ♃ 7:15
☽ ⚼ ☿ 8:13
☿ // ♅ 8:19
♀ □ ♆ 11:15
♂ ⚹ ♇ 5:21PM
☉ # ☿ 5:44
☽ # ♀ 8:17

positive for beginning projects involving communication, transportation, electronic media, technology in general, and on higher octaves, magic. The second easily brings problems to relationships, especially where intoxicants are overindulged and the otherwise spaced are involved. Be on the lookout for confusion, misunderstanding, and a willingness to fight over it. Don't. The third can be very positive for any activity involving the use of energy and power. This can easily be used behind the scenes and much may be accomplished while most people remain unaware. Be nice. The fourth is positive for looking within and coming to deeper self-understanding. The fifth, which peaks in tomorrow's late predawn, is very positive for any sort of activity involving prayer, meditation, or other spiritual practices. Be open to the intuitive process and pay attention to your dreams.

Thursday, 5th

☽ ∠ ♇ 1:48
☿ ⚺ ♆ 2:35
☽ ⚻ ☉ 4:30
☉ # ♅ 6:01
☽ △ ♅ 6:42
☽ □ ♄ 10:36
☽ ⚺ ♃ 1:30PM
☽ // ♃ 2:28
☽ □ ♆ 4:44
♃ ℞ 6:23
☽ △ ☿ 6:42
☽ ☍ ♀ 7:54

High energy from the past few days both positive and otherwise will remain with us through today. Continue to be open to the intuitive process and follow guidance. There is another major energy that can go either way. On the downside, watch for erratic and bizarre behavior of all kinds. The nutcases will be on parade. Also watch for problems with and for authority. On the upside, this energy can be very good for understanding and making good use of technology and magic. Watch the early to mid predawn for a brief period of coercive irritability. The late predawn also has erratic emotional reactions. Take an innovative approach through the morning, but watch the late morning for a period of hard attitudes. An expansive approach will serve best through the afternoon. The late afternoon through early evening is mixed. Watch for spaciness while positive communication follows, only to give way to potential relationship issues. Choices. Also be aware that the Moon will be void of course from 7:54 tonight well into tomorrow morning.

Friday, 6th

♂ – ♓ 1:49
☽ ⚺ ♇ 7:51
☉ ⚺ ♅ 8:29
☽ – ♐ 9:56
☽ □ ♂ 10:29
☽ ⚼ ☉ 1:12PM

Last night's Moon void of course period ends at 9:56 this morning when the Moon enters Sagittarius. At that point the energy will lift noticeably and general moods will tend to become more expansive and open to a wide range of ideas. There are two major energies today. The first indicates a general shift in the way energy and power are approached to a more intangible understanding. The second is a continu-

April 2007   Pacific Time

ation of yesterday's energy, but in a more positive form. Make good use of it. There may be a brief period of aggressiveness following the void of course and some very minor irritability in the early afternoon. This should be a fun and enjoyable Friday night as a positive, social and relationship energy peaking tomorrow morning rolls in.

Saturday, 7th

☿	✶	♀	9:06
☽	□	♅	6:32PM
☽	△	☉	9:20
☽	△	♄	9:57

Late Friday night social scenes will be energized well into today's predawn. The positive social and relationship energy mentioned yesterday will remain very much with us through today. Make a friendly gesture in an appropriate situation and it may well be reciprocated. There is another major energy coming into focus throughout the day that is very positive for situations involving self-discipline, authority, older people, and traditional matters. This is part of a very positive complex running through the next couple of days. Seek to improve things across the board. Good moods should run through the late night and this will be an active, social Saturday night.

Sunday, 8th

☽	☌	♃	12:51
☽	✶	♆	4:07
☉	△	♄	4:55
☽	⊼	♀	1:15PM
☽	□	☿	2:13
☽	☌	♇	6:34
☽	—	♑	8:35

Great positive energy continues through today. Work toward firming the foundations that your life is built upon. Make improvements in all the things that matter most to you. Pay attention to the multigenerational relationships in your family and in the rest of your life. Understand that your freedom is limited only by the degree of your self-discipline. Late Saturday night social situations will remain active in today's predawn. The morning should be primarily positive. Watch the early afternoon for minor relationship issues and irritability. This will pass quickly. Be aware that the Moon will be void of course this evening from 6:34 until 8:35 when it will enter Capricorn. At that point the energy will lift and general moods will tend to become more down to earth and concerned with accomplishment.

Monday, 9th

☽	✶	♂	12:55
☽	⊓	♄	2:48
☽	∠	♆	8:55
☉	△	♃	5:06PM
☽	⊓	♀	8:38

The positive energy from the past few days continues very strongly through today. Take an expansive approach to the improvements previously recommended. There is another major energy coming into focus today, however, that is more cautionary. Watch for problems in communication and transportation, especially where coerciveness and just plain nasty attitudes are indulged. This energy also leads to the exposure of things normally kept secret and hidden.

Astro-Weather

Pacific Time   April 2007

Guard your secrets and keep the eyes and ears open as there will be much to learn. This will definitely be a day for good choices.

Tuesday, 10th

☿	□	♇	12:24
☽	⚹	♅	3:57
☽	∠	♂	6:53
☽	⊼	♄	6:54
☽	⚻	♃	9:40
☽	□	☉	11:02
☽	⚻	♆	12:55PM
☿	—	♈	4:06
♀	⊼	♇	9:32

The high positive energy from the past few days will tend to linger through today. Watch, however, for yesterday's cautionary energy to remain with us as well. There are two more major energies running through today. The first indicates a general shift in communication and transportation toward a more assertive and aggressive mode. The second is highly cautionary and easily leads to a heavy and potentially coercive sexuality. While this can be fun for some, it can be unsettling and even dangerous for others. This particular configuration brings the energy up unexpectedly and seemingly out of nowhere. As always with this energy, protect the vulnerable. Minor aspects are mixed at best throughout the day, and you will want to watch the late morning through midday for a period of intensely bad moods.

Wednesday, 11th

☽	⚻	♆	2:27
☽	△	♀	2:56
☽	—	♒	4:22
☽	⚹	☿	6:05
☽	∠	♅	7:25
☽	⚻	♂	11:49
☉	⚹	♆	12:33PM
☽	∠	♃	12:50
☽	∥	♃	1:06
☽	#	♀	5:32
♀	—	♊	7:14

Continue to observe yesterday's cautionary energy all the way through today. There are two more major energies running through today. The first is very positive for any sort of prayer, meditation, or other spiritual practice one may be involved in. Be open to the intuitive process and follow guidance as it occurs. The second indicates a general shift in relationship energy toward a more communicative mode. There will be a short Moon void of course period this morning from 2:56 until 4:22 when the Moon enters Aquarius. At that point the energy will lift and general moods will tend to become more independent and free-thinking. Moods should be positive through the predawn. The rest of the day is mixed, but good moods should predominate. Watch the early evening for some potential minor relationship issues.

Thursday, 12th

☽	∠	♆	5:05
☽	⚻	♅	9:59
☽	∠	☿	12:10PM
☽	☍	♄	12:29
☿	□	♄	2:44
☽	⚹	♃	3:05
☽	#	♄	5:00
☽	∥	♆	5:50
☽	☌	♆	6:17

There is a major energy running throughout today that can bring problems to communication and transportation. Watch for people running into restrictions and frustrations, and acting out on them. Don't get caught up in this, as consequences can be harsher and longer-lasting than usual. Most of today's predawn is open. Watch the late predawn for a brief period of coercive irritability. This will pass quickly and most of the morning is open. Take an innovative approach through the late morning but watch the midday for

Astro-Weather   49

☽	⚹	☉	8:27

minor irritability and hard attitudes. The rest of the afternoon is more positive. Take a disciplined approach through the late afternoon and enjoy good mood energy into the late night.

Friday, 13th

☽	//	♆	1:34
☽	⚹	♇	6:49
☽	→	♓	8:37
☽	□	♀	11:57
☽	//	♂	4:52PM
☽	⚺	☿	5:06
☽	☌	♂	6:31
☽	#	☉	9:44
☽	∠	☉	11:32

Today's predawn is open for the most part, but it will be a good idea to be open to the intuitive process and pay special attention to dreams. The Moon will be void of course this morning from 6:49 until 8:37 when it will enter Pisces. At that point the energy will lift and general moods will tend to become more mellow, if a bit spacy. Most of the rest of the morning following the void of course is open, but watch the midday for relationship issues. Take an active approach through the rest of the afternoon into the evening and be open to positive communication. Late night social scenes will become more intense as a highly social energy that peaks tomorrow morning comes more into focus.

Saturday, 14th

♀	#	♃	8:39
☽	//	♅	9:47
☽	☌	♅	12:33PM
☿	⚺	♂	1:36
☽	⚻	♄	2:42
☿	∠	♆	2:45
☽	□	♃	5:06
☽	⚺	♆	8:15

Late Friday night social scenes will be very highly energized through today's predawn. This high social energy will remain with us through today and tonight. It is joined by two more major energies. The first is very good for any activity involving communication, transportation, and the use of energy and power. The second, however, is more cautionary. Watch for the inebriated and otherwise out of it. Be especially careful in traffic. Aside from the major energies, take an innovative and fun approach through the morning and much of the afternoon. Watch the mid through late afternoon for hard attitudes and exaggerated emotional reactions. The late night becomes more positive, and this will be another high energy, social Saturday night.

Sunday, 15th

☽	⚺	☉	1:45
☽	#	☿	3:01
☽	□	♇	8:01
☽	//	☿	9:12
☽	→	♈	9:45
☽	⚼	♄	2:49PM
☽	⚹	♀	5:03
☽	∠	♆	8:19
☽	⚺	♂	9:46
☉	#	♂	10:23

There is a major energy running throughout the day that is very good for increasing understanding and the uses of energy and power. Good moods should run through most of today's predawn. There may be a brief period of minor irritability in the mid predawn but this will pass quickly, if it is noticed at all. The Moon will be void of course this morning from 8:01 until 9:45 when it will enter Aries. At that point the energy will lift and general moods will tend to become more assertive and aggressive. Watch the mid afternoon for a brief period of hard attitudes. Once past this, moods will improve through the rest of the afternoon to the early evening. There may be some minor spaciness in the later evening, but this will give way once again to more positive moods.

Monday, 16th

☽	☌	☿	12:07
☽	#	♅	1:24
☽	⚺	♅	12:39PM
☽	△	♄	2:33
☽	#	♂	2:55
☽	//	☉	4:30
☽	△	♃	4:48
☽	∠	♀	6:43
☽	⚹	♆	8:02
☽	∠	♂	10:42

Yesterday's major energy will remain with us through today. You will notice energy levels rising today as another major energy, tomorrow morning's new Moon, rolls in. Consider today, tomorrow, and Wednesday to be the new Moon period. Be good at the very least, and think in terms of making positive changes. Today's early predawn is mixed. A communicative approach will serve best, but watch for some erratic emotional reactions. The morning is open. Good moods are likely to run through most of the afternoon. Be open to innovation, yet take a disciplined approach. There may be some minor aggressiveness in the mid afternoon, but this will pass quickly and good moods should run through the evening for those who don't get caught up in minor relationship issues. Remember the new Moon and make good choices.

Tuesday, 17th

☽	☌	☉	4:36
☽	△	♇	7:26
☽	#	♆	7:58
☽	—	♉	9:11
☽	∠	♅	12:19PM
☽	#	♇	3:14
☽	//	♄	4:05
☽	⚼	♃	4:21
☽	⚺	♀	8:17
☽	⚹	♂	11:34

Today is new Moon day. It is exact at 4:36 this morning. Remember that what you start around new Moon tends to bring results at the next full Moon. During this particular new to full period, it will be a good idea to focus on positive self-transformation. There may be some aggressiveness in the early predawn, but this will pass quickly and the rest of the predawn through the early morning is open. Take a co-operative approach in the morning, but you will have to work around the Moon void of course period running from 7:26 until 9:11 when the Moon enters Taurus. At that point the energy will lift noticeably and general moods will tend to become more down to earth and concerned with enjoyment. There is scattered minor irritability from the midday through much of the afternoon and into the early evening. Moods will become more positive later.

Wednesday, 18th

☽	⚺	☿	5:42
☽	⚼	♇	7:05
☽	⚹	♅	12:06PM
☽	□	♄	1:52
☽	⚻	♃	4:02
☽	#	♃	5:09
☽	□	♆	7:29

Consider the new Moon to run through today and continue to make the right choices. There is a major energy coming into focus today that is very positive for seeing more deeply. Light will be shed on things normally beneath the surface, but not in a confrontational or negative way. It will be much easier to make needed changes. Good moods should run through the predawn. There may be some minor irrita-

April 2007 — Pacific Time

☽	∥	♀	11:51

bility and coerciveness in the early morning, but this will pass quickly. Moods will be mixed from the midday through much of the afternoon. Take a fun approach and be open to innovation, but watch for hard attitudes and feelings of lack or restriction. Take an expansive approach through the late afternoon and early evening, but watch for spaciness and be aware that the Moon will be void of course from 7:29 tonight well into tomorrow morning.

Thursday, 19th

☉	△	♇	12:34
☽	⚻	♇	7:02
☽	⚺	☉	7:30
☽	–	♊	8:51
☽	∠	☿	9:02
♄	D		2:25PM

Last night's Moon void of course period ends at 8:51 this morning when the Moon enters Gemini. At that point the energy will lift noticeably and general moods will tend to become more communicative. The high positive energy from yesterday will remain with us through today and will be especially available after the void of course ends. There may be a brief period of irritability following the void of course, but this may pass unnoticed. The rest of the day through the late night is open. Make good use of it.

Friday, 20th

☽	☌	♀	12:28
☽	□	♂	2:25
☉	–	♉	4:07
☽	∠	☉	9:50
☿	⚺	♅	11:09
☽	□	♅	1:01PM
☽	✶	☿	1:17
☽	✶	♄	2:43
☽	☍	♃	4:50
☽	△	♆	8:43

There are three major energies today. The first is the Sun's entry into the fixed earth sign Taurus. During this time, work to solidify the beginnings made back at the Vernal Equinox. Nurture those little seedlings. The second is very positive for activities involving communication and transportation, especially where electricity and electronic media are involved. This energy also works very well for dealing with technology and magic. The third is also very positive for any activity involving communication and transportation, and is excellent for negotiation and coming to long-term agreement. There may be some minor aggression in the mid predawn, a brief period of irritability in the mid to late morning, and the early afternoon may have a short burst of erratic emotional responses. Aside from those brief interludes, moods should be uncommonly good and it should be possible to accomplish a great deal. This will be an active social Friday night. Have fun, but be mindful of the important things.

Saturday, 21st

☿	△	♄	12:08
☽	☍	♆	8:53
☽	–	♋	10:51
☿	#	♅	11:01
☽	✶	☉	1:10PM

High positive energy for communication and transportation remains very much with us through today. There are two more major energies related to this. The first can be somewhat cautionary as some people will simply fry out on the abundance of it. Watch for some erratic and bizarre behav-

Pacific Time   April 2007

☿ △ ♃   3:38
☽ ∠ ♄   4:18
☽ ⚼ ♆   10:35

...ior and be especially careful in traffic as some people will be getting carried away. The second simply continues the abundance of positivity. The predawn is open and positive. There may be some minor coercive irritability in the mid morning, and you will want to be aware that the Moon will be void of course this morning from 8:53 until 10:51 when it will enter Cancer. At that point the energy will lift and general moods will tend to become more sensitive and protective. Aside from a brief period of potential hard attitudes in the late afternoon, good moods will predominate and this should be a fun, social Saturday night.

Sunday, 22nd

☽ ⚻ ♀   8:19
☽ △ ♂   8:45
☉ ∠ ♅   10:51
☽ △ ♅   5:13PM
☽ ⚻ ♄   6:55
☽ ⚼ ♃   9:01
☿ ⚹ ♆   9:10
♀ □ ♂   10:30

Make good choices and seek to keep the glow from the past few days going. There are three more major energies running through the day, two of which are much more cautionary. The first brings out the crazies. Watch for the nutballs, who will be out in force. The second continues the positive energy. This aspect is excellent for any prayer, meditation, or spiritual activities one may be involved in. Be open to the intuitive process and follow guidance. Focus on the second energy as the third easily stimulates conflict in relationships. It would be a shame to waste all the positive energy on some silly fight. Try not to think it, and certainly don't say it. Avoiding the difficult energies, good moods should dominate the day. Choose.

Monday, 23rd

☽ ⚼ ♆   1:27
☽ □ ☿   2:11
☽ ∥ ♀   11:28
☽ ⚼ ♂   1:42PM
☽ ∠ ♀   2:12
☽ ⚼ ♇   2:28
☽ – ☊   4:38
☿ # ♂   8:26
☽ ⚼ ♅   8:55
☽ □ ☉   11:36

Yesterday's energy for conflict in relationships will tend to linger through today. Resist any temptation to indulge. There is another major energy coming into focus through the day that can stimulate problems in communication and transportation, especially where people become impatient and pushy. Watch for those trying to say and do too much, and becoming frustrated. Be especially careful in traffic. All of this may be tempered somewhat by the long Moon void of course period which runs from 2:11 this morning until 4:38 this afternoon when the Moon enters Leo. At that point the energy will lift noticeably and general moods will tend to become more intense and concerned with self. Try to take it easy through the void of course and tend to old business. Moods should be open following the void of course through the evening, but watch the late night for a downturn and the potential for very bad moods.

Astro-Weather

April 2007   Pacific Time

☽	⚻	♃	12:38
☽	#	♃	1:38
☉	⚻	♃	12:16PM
☽	⚻	♇	6:48
☽	⚺	♂	7:54
☽	✶	♀	9:26

Tuesday, 24th

There is a major energy running throughout today that is much more positive than otherwise, but still bears watching. People will tend to optimism and generally feeling good about themselves. Problems come in where people get carried away and ego battles may result. Make use of the positivity, but keep a grip. Watch the early predawn for a period of intensely bad moods. Try to take an expansive approach through the rest of the predawn. Aside from the major energy, the daytime is open. Watch the evening for irritability and erratic emotional responses, but the late night becomes more positive.

☽	⚺	♅	1:36
☽	☌	♄	3:14
☽	△	♃	5:11
☽	∥	♄	7:59
☽	#	♇	9:02
☽	⚼	♆	10:17
☽	#	♆	6:17PM
☽	△	☿	10:00
☽	∥	☉	11:12

Wednesday, 25th

Watch today's early predawn for a brief period of erratic emotional reactions. Take a disciplined approach through the mid predawn. The late predawn to early morning becomes much more positive and an expansive attitude will serve best. Maintain a disciplined approach. Watch the early to mid morning for minor coerciveness and spaciness. Aside from a brief period of spaciness in the very early evening, the rest of the afternoon through the nighttime is open. Moods will improve in the very late night.

☽	△	♇	12:02
☽	—	♍	2:24
☿	△	♇	10:05
☽	∥	☿	2:19PM
☽	△	☉	2:54
♀	□	♅	8:20

Thursday, 26th

There are two major energies running throughout today. The first is very positive for looking within and beneath the surface, and coming to deeper understanding. Things normally kept secret and hidden will become more apparent, but not in a negative or difficult way. Observe, learn, teach, and evolve. The second is rather more cautionary. This energy easily brings about problems in relationships. Watch for sudden, unrealistic, and unreasonable demands for change. Erratic behavior should be avoided. If trouble pops up in this area, switch to damage control and ride it out. The predawn should start out with positive moods, but be aware that the Moon will be void of course from 12:02 until 2:24 when it will enter Virgo. At that point the energy will lift and general moods will tend to become more discerning and concerned with detail. Aside from the major energies, moods should be much more positive than otherwise, especially through the afternoon and early evening.

☿	—	♉	12:15
☽	#	♂	4:44

Friday, 27th

Continue to observe the cautionary energy from yesterday through today. There are three more major energies to be

Astro-Weather

☽	#	♅	9:28
☽	⚼	☿	10:04
☽	☍	♂	11:12
♀	⚹	♄	1:06PM
☽	☍	♅	1:18
☽	⚺	♄	2:51
☽	□	♀	3:02
☽	□	♃	4:31
☿	∠	♂	7:51
☽	⚻	♆	10:11
☽	⚼	☉	11:46

aware of. The first indicates a general shift in thinking and communicating toward a more down-to-earth mode. The second is very positive for relationships and will be a very welcome energy for those caught up in the past couple days' relationship nonsense. This energy is excellent for strengthening and solidifying relationships. The third can bring problems to communication and transportation, especially where people become frustrated and pushy. In extreme cases, this can escalate all the way to violence. Be especially careful in traffic and offer no single-digit salutes. Minor aspects are mixed at best through the day, so good choices are in order. This will be a high-energy, social Friday night, however, as an intense party aspect, exact tomorrow morning, comes into focus.

Saturday, 28th

☿	∠	♅	5:02
♀	☍	♃	5:43
☽	□	♇	12:14PM
☽	→	♎	2:44
☽	∠	♄	9:19
♂	☌	♅	9:36
☿	⚼	♃	10:06
☽	⚻	☿	10:55

High energy from yesterday, both positive and otherwise, will continue through today and is joined by four more major energies. The first continues yesterday's cautionary communication and transportation energy and adds electronic media and technology issues to the frustration. Don't try to fix your computer with a hammer. The second is the intensely social energy mentioned yesterday that easily leads to all manner of overindulgence. Have fun, but ... The third is very good for beginning any project involving the use of energy, power, technology, and magic. The fourth is once again problematic for communication and transportation. Don't bite off more than you can chew or make promises you can't deliver on. Be aware that the Moon will be void of course this afternoon from 12:14 until 2:44 when it enters Libra. At that point the energy will lift and general moods will tend to become more concerned with balance and beauty. This will again be a highly social Saturday night. Take care.

Sunday, 29th

☽	⚼	♆	4:40
☉	#	♆	6:47
☽	⚻	☉	8:58
☽	//	♅	9:39
☽	//	♂	11:41
☿	∠	♀	6:35PM
♂	⚻	♄	9:09

The high energy just keeps on rolling with today offering three more major energies to go along with the carry-over from the past few days. The first brings out the space cases. Watch for the inebriated and otherwise out of it. If you meet someone who seems a sandwich short of a picnic, they probably are. The second stirs up controversy in relationships. If you have the slightest inkling that it may not be a good idea to say it, don't. The third, which dovetails quite nicely with the second, is a great deal more cautionary. Disputes of any kind can easily spiral out of control, with

April 2007   Pacific Time

consequences much harsher and longer-lasting than usual. Do not let minor issues become major. Backing off is sometimes the wiser of available options. Minor aspects are of no help and good choices are imperative.

Monday, 30th

☽ ⊼ ♅	2:25
☽ ✶ ♄	3:52
☽ ⊼ ♂	4:19
☽ ✶ ♃	5:05
☽ △ ♀	10:26
☽ △ ♆	11:12
♂ □ ♃	3:21PM
♀ △ ♆	6:33
☽ # ☿	10:27

No respite from the high energy. Continue to observe all of the cautions from yesterday. There are three more major energies to deal with today. The first enhances the third from yesterday. This is an excess of energy itself. While there is a tremendous amount of energy that can be used positively, many will find it difficult to contain and use properly. Be on the lookout for altercations of all kinds and don't get caught in anyone else's crossfire. The second can be very positive for taking relationships to more spiritual levels. This energy can also be used socially, and that is how most people will approach it. Better to party than to fight. Just make sure that one doesn't lead to the other. Aside from the major energies, good moods should run through most of the day. Choose well.

May 2007

Overview

This will be a month to remember. As May begins, the Jupiter, Saturn, Uranus and Neptune complex that took shape last month is very strong, with Venus and Mars also briefly involved. Few people will not be, or at least feel, caught up in all of this energy. There are too many individual aspects to isolate out of this and call dominant. What you will see is tremendous activity going in all directions, and factions on all sides will see their fortunes rise and fall in dizzying succession. The Venus connection will fade in just a few days and Mars will remain a few days longer. These separations will make it all seem somewhat less personal, but the first week or so will be very intense, especially the first weekend. As the month wears on, Jupiter will begin to retro back out of all of this. It will remain in orb, but the fade will begin and this is not really the best of news. Jupiter's involvement has been to the positive and this will leave us mostly to the rougher energies. Saturn even manages a contra-parallel to Pluto on the 18th which is related to the original 9/11 energy. Things are likely to become harsher later in the month and all the light that can be generated will be needed. Please do what you can to participate in whatever global prayer and meditation for peace events get organized.

This will be a very high energy month on the more personal levels as well. This is partly due to the unusual involvement of Venus and Mars in the above mentioned configuration. The first weekend is a doozy and you will want to be vigilant for several days on either side of it. The second weekend has quite cautionary energies as well. There are a great deal of high energy aspects both cautionary and positive throughout the month. The single most significant long daytime Moon void of course period is on the 3rd.

Tuesday, 1st

☽	⚹	♇	1:06
☽	//	♆	1:46
☽	–	♏	3:40
♂	//	♅	3:45
☽	#	☉	4:37
☽	⚼	♅	8:56
☽	∠	♃	11:17
☽	//	♇	11:26
☽	#	♄	12:24PM

Watch for fallout from the past few days to linger through today. Continue to observe the cautions. There are two more major energies. The first, on higher octaves, can be very positive for any prayer, meditation, or spiritual activities one may be involved in. At lower octaves, however, it brings out the space cases. Watch for a greater incidence of confusion and misunderstanding. Be on the lookout for the inebriated and otherwise out of it, and be especially careful in traffic. You will notice energy levels rising throughout

May 2007

Pacific Time

☽	⛝	♂	12:47
☿	#	♆	6:09
☽	⛝	♀	7:58

the day as the full Moon rolls in. It is exact in tomorrow's late predawn, making tonight effectively full Moon. Remember that full Moons are always high energy and deserve to be approached with respect. This particular full Moon is best used for solidifying positive changes initiated back at the previous new Moon. There will be a relatively short Moon void of course period this morning from 1:06 until 3:40 when the Moon enters Scorpio. At that point the energy will lift and general moods will tend to become more intense. Minor aspects are of very little help through the day and good choices will be needed.

Wednesday, 2nd

☽	☍	☿	12:59
☽	☍	☉	3:09
☽	⚼	♆	7:18
☽	△	♅	3:11PM
☽	□	♄	4:31
☽	⚺	♃	5:14
☽	//	♃	8:18
☽	△	♂	8:58
☉	♂	☿	9:05
☽	□	♆	11:41

The full Moon is exact at 3:09 this morning. Consider the full Moon to run very strongly through today and tomorrow at least. Reread. There is another major energy coming into focus throughout the day that is very good for looking within and coming to greater self-understanding. Aside from the major energy, today's early predawn may have a brief period of argumentativeness. Watch the early morning for a brief period of coercive irritability, which may well pass unnoticed. Most of the rest of the daytime is open, with moods improving especially through the mid afternoon. The late afternoon through early evening is mixed. Avoid any temptation to indulge in hard attitudes and take an expansive and active approach right on into the late night. Do be aware that the Moon will be void of course from 11:41 tonight through much of tomorrow.

Thursday, 3rd

☉	//	☿	4:49
☽	⚻	♀	5:07
☿	⛝	♆	11:51
☽	⚺	♆	1:11PM
☽	–	♐	3:47
☽	#	♀	11:24

The energy for looking within mentioned yesterday will remain with us through today. There is a related aspect running through today that deepens and adds a more cautionary element. Guard your secrets and keep the eyes and ears open as there will be much to learn. Last night's Moon void of course runs through much of today and ends at 3:47 this afternoon when the Moon enters Sagittarius. At that point the energy will lift very noticeably and general moods will tend to become more expansive and open to a wide range of ideas. Relax and take it easy through the void of course as best you can, and focus on cleaning up old business.

Friday, 4th

☿	#	♆	2:58
☉	⛝	♆	5:40
☿	//	♄	8:07

The cautionary energy mentioned yesterday will run very strongly through today and is enhanced by yet another energy that is much the same. Light will be shed on things

Pacific Time May 2007

♂	⚹	♆	4:31PM
☽	⚻	☉	7:49

☽	⚻	☿	1:19
☽	□	♅	2:38
☽	△	♄	3:52
☽	☌	♃	4:03
☿	⚹	♅	8:53
☽	⚹	♆	10:46
☽	□	♂	11:57
☿	□	♄	3:54PM
☿	⚻	♃	4:20
☉	#	♇	6:47
☽	☍	♀	9:49
☽	☌	♇	11:44

♃	△	♄	12:09
☽	–	♑	2:20
☽	⚼	☉	3:21
☉	∥	♄	7:57
☽	⚼	♄	8:52
☽	⚼	☿	12:20PM
☽	∠	♆	3:37
♀	☍	♇	7:05

normally kept secret and hidden. This energy also can bring problems with and for authority. Watch for moves toward regime change today and tomorrow. There is another major energy that on higher octaves is very positive for any spiritual activity one may be involved in. This energy can also be used socially, and of course that is how most people will respond. This will be a high energy Friday night. Have fun but watch for some minor irritability.

Saturday, 5th

Cautionary energy mentioned the past two days will remain with us through today. There are five more major energies that are contradictory. The first is very positive for communication and transportation, especially where electricity and electronic media are involved. The second can easily bring problems to communication and transportation, especially where people run into restrictions and frustrations, and act out on them. The third aggravates the situation by stimulating a great deal of erratic activity in communication and transportation. Best case people manage themselves and get a lot done. Worst case people try to say and do too much, run into roadblocks, react badly, and the situation explodes. Choices may be in order here. The fourth adds fuel to the fire of the cautionary energy above. Keep an eye on motives, others' as well as your own. The fifth is a long range outer planet aspect that tends to generate more stability in the outer world. With good choices, this can be a good day. Do your best. Be aware that the Moon will be void of course from 11:44 tonight into tomorrow's predawn.

Sunday, 6th

Last night's Moon void of course period ends at 2:20 this morning when the Moon enters Capricorn. At that point the energy will lift and general moods will tend to become more down to earth and concerned with accomplishment. High energy from the past few days will continue through today and you will want to observe all of the cautions. There are three more major energies to deal with today that are of very little help. The first is the most positive and should be used to initiate projects involving self-understanding and self-discipline. The second easily stimulates a heavy and potentially coercive sexuality. This is one of the strongest configurations of this energy, and while it can be fun for some, it can be quite dangerous for others. As always with this energy, protect the vulnerable. The third, which actually peaks tomorrow morning, brings more prob-

May 2007   Pacific Time

☿	□	♆	7:28
☽	△	☉	10:11
☽	✶	♅	12:10PM
☽	⚻	♃	12:59
☽	⚼	♄	1:19
☽	#	♀	4:34
☽	⚻	♆	7:53
☽	△	☿	10:21

♀	→	♋	12:28
☽	✶	♂	12:33
☽	⚻	♆	8:13
☽	→	♒	10:46
☽	⚼	♀	11:44
☉	✶	♅	1:24PM
☽	∠	♅	4:03
☽	∠	♃	4:34
☿	✶	♂	5:38
☽	∥	♃	7:21
☉	⚼	♃	8:10

☉	□	♄	5:05
☽	∠	♂	5:44

lems to communication and transportation, especially where inebriants and the otherwise out of it are involved. Watch for spaciness and confusion, and be especially careful in traffic.

Monday, 7th

Cautionary energy mentioned yesterday involving spaciness and confusion will remain very much with us through today. Remember to be careful in traffic and watch for the space cases who will be out in force. Aside from the major energy, the predawn through most of the morning is open to do with as you will. Moods will become much more positive from the mid morning through the midday. There may be a brief downturn in the early afternoon with erratic hard attitudes and the late afternoon may have another brief period of irritability and relationship issues. Once past this, moods will again swing to the positive. Enjoy.

Tuesday, 8th

The Moon will be void of course this morning from 12:33 until 10:46 when it enters Aquarius. At that point the energy will lift noticeably and general moods will tend to become more independent and free-thinking. There are five major energies running throughout today. Once again they are largely contradictory. The first indicates a general shift in relationship energy toward a more sensitive and protective mode. The second can be very positive for any activity involving technology, science, and on higher octaves, magic. This energy can also be used for fun. The third is also positive for any activity involving communication, transportation, and the uses of energy and power. Much may be learned in these areas, and this energy should be taken advantage of. The fourth contradicts the second. While it does stimulate feelings of positivity and well-being, it also easily leads to overindulgence of all kinds and inflated egos. Watch for people getting carried away and running into the fifth major energy, which easily leads to feelings of restriction and frustration, with unfortunate acting out. This will definitely be a day to make wise choices, as running afoul of the difficult energy can lead to much harsher and longer-lasting consequences than usual. Be especially careful in your dealings with authority.

Wednesday, 9th

High energy from yesterday will linger through today. Reread and apply both the positive indications and the caution-

Pacific Time   May 2007

☽	#	☿	6:21
☽	∠	♇	11:29
☽	□	♀	5:24PM
☽	⚼	♅	7:13
☽	✶	♃	7:27
☽	#	☉	7:30
☽	☍	♄	8:18
☽	□	☉	9:25
☽	#	♄	11:57

ary. The last major energy mentioned yesterday will be the strongest through today. Continue to be very careful in your dealings with and for authority, older people, and traditional matters. This will not be the day to smart off to the boss or the judge or the cop writing you the ticket. Aside from the major energy, most of the predawn is open. Watch the late predawn through midday for scattered minor aggressiveness, irritability, and coercion. Most of the afternoon opens up but watch the late afternoon for a brief period of relationship issues. This will pass quickly and moods will improve for two or three hours but then nosedive. Be prepared for the switch and don't be caught unaware. The later evening through the late night has hard attitudes and a period of intensely bad moods. An early bedtime might be the best idea.

Thursday, 10th

☽	∥	♇	12:29
☽	☌	♆	2:25
☽	∥	♆	8:58
☿	⚻	♇	9:57
☽	⚼	♂	10:01
☽	✶	♇	2:01PM
☽	□	☿	2:45
☽	—	♓	4:31
♃	□	♅	8:31
☽	△	♀	10:04

There are three major energies running throughout the day. The first easily leads to the exposure of secret and coercive activities. There will be a great deal of activity beneath the surface and observation will yield learning. This energy also stimulates difficulty in communication and transportation where sarcasm and nasty attitudes are indulged. Be careful in traffic and don't let minor disputes escalate. The second is a long range outer planet aspect that serves to keep the international conflict going. Watch the news for spectacular headlines. The third, which peaks early tomorrow morning, easily brings problems to relationships. Watch for cold, hard attitudes and unreasonableness. If trouble pops up, switch to damage control as consequences of indulging in this energy can be harsher and longer lasting than usual. The Moon will be void of course this afternoon from 2:45 until 4:31 when it enters Pisces. At that point the energy will lift and general moods will tend to become more mellow, if a bit spacy.

Friday, 11th

☿	→	♊	2:17
♀	∠	♄	5:59
☽	∥	♅	7:31PM
☽	□	♃	11:02
☽	☌	♅	11:16

There are two major energies running through today. The first is Mercury's entry into its own sign, Gemini, which indicates an increase in energy for communication and transportation. The second is the harsh relationship energy mentioned yesterday which will remain with us through today. Aside from the major energies, the day is largely open. Have fun tonight, but be mindful of the cautionary relationship energy.

Saturday, 12th

☽	⚻	♄	12:19
☽	⚹	☉	5:01
☽	⚺	♆	6:01
☽	//	♂	6:48
☿	#	♃	12:17PM
☽	☌	♂	4:00
☽	□	♇	4:53
☽	→	♈	7:18
☉	□	♆	7:55
☽	#	♂	10:01

There are two major energies running throughout today. The first will stimulate a great deal of activity around communication and transportation. Based on this energy alone, this would be a go-for-it day in which much may be accomplished. This can still be the case, but today's second major energy will need to be handled correctly. This aspect easily leads to a great deal of spaciness and confusion. Watch for the space cases who will be out in full force. If you see someone who seems to be a thimble short of a sewing kit, they almost certainly are. Be on the lookout for the inebriated, and those off-their-meds. Aside from the major energy, the early predawn may be a little tricky and late Friday-nighters may want to pack it in early. The late pre-dawn through early morning is much more positive. The rest of the morning through much of the afternoon is open. Watch the late afternoon for a period of irritability and coerciveness, and be aware that the Moon will be void of course from 4:53 until 7:18 tonight when it enters Aries. At that point the energy will lift and general moods will tend to become more assertive and aggressive. Have fun tonight, but remember the cautionary energy and be careful.

Sunday, 13th

☽	⚼	♄	1:17
☽	⚹	☿	2:01
☽	□	♀	4:40
☽	∠	♆	6:46
☽	∠	☉	7:31
♂	□	♇	8:15
☽	#	♅	9:36
☽	△	♃	11:59PM

There is a major energy running throughout the day that is among the very most cautionary. Late Saturday night party people will need to be especially careful. This energy easily leads to secret and coercive violence and there will be an undercurrent that should not be ignored. Under no circumstances allow yourself to be drawn into altercations with strangers. Do not let any disputes escalate, as violence that does occur can be especially damaging. This is not an energy to play around with, as those who do run afoul of it will not soon forget what happens. Minor aspects are of little to no help, and this is definitely a day for good choices.

Monday, 14th

☽	⚺	♅	12:39
☽	△	♄	1:41
☽	∠	☿	6:06
☽	⚹	♆	7:01
♀	⚼	♆	9:12
☽	⚺	☉	9:25
☽	△	♇	5:23PM
☿	⚺	♀	5:48
☽	#	♆	5:59

The high cautionary energy mentioned yesterday will remain very much with us through today. Reread yesterday and apply carefully. There are two more major energies running through the day. The first easily leads to spaciness and confusion in relationships, especially where intoxicants and the otherwise out of it are involved. This is in bad combination with the cautionary energy mentioned above. Be very careful not to indulge in tantrums and overreactions to perceived slights by those close to you, as things can so easily

Pacific Time   May 2007

☽ ☌ ♂	7:12
☽ – ♉	7:48
☽ □ ♃	11:48

spiral out of control and unfortunate things occur before one has a chance to pull back. The second, very fortunately, is very positive for communication in relationships. This is the energy to focus on. Remain calm, rational, and seek only greater balance. Situations that require winners and losers are the most likely to explode. Minor aspects are mixed, but are more positive than otherwise and good choices can easily be made. Make them. Do be aware that the Moon will be void of course from 5:23 this afternoon until 7:48 tonight when it enters Taurus. At that point the energy will lift and general moods will tend to become more down to earth and concerned with enjoyment.

Tuesday, 15th

☽ ∠ ♅	12:42
☽ # ♆	1:44
☽ // ♄	1:57
♂ – ♈	7:06
☽ ✶ ♀	8:38
☽ ☌ ☿	9:36
☽ // ☉	12:21PM
☽ □ ♇	5:13
☽ ∠ ♂	8:19
☽ ⚻ ♃	11:29

Fallout from the past few days may linger through today. Be kind to those licking wounds and be on the lookout for holdouts who have not let go of issues. There is another major energy running through the day that indicates a general shift in the uses of energy and power toward a more assertive mode. This is Mars entering its own sign, Aries. You will notice energy levels rising throughout the day as tomorrow's new Moon rolls in. It is exact in the early afternoon, but you will want to consider the new Moon period as starting today. Be good. Aside from the major energies, there is scattered minor irritability in the early through mid predawn. The late predawn to early morning opens up and good moods will run through the rest of the morning. Most of the afternoon is open but watch the late afternoon for a brief period of minor coercive irritability. This will pass quickly but there may be some aggressiveness in the later evening. Choose well.

Wednesday, 16th

☽ ✶ ♅	12:35
☽ □ ♄	1:39
☽ # ♃	3:20
☽ □ ♆	6:48
☽ ∠ ♀	10:20
☽ ☌ ☉	12:27PM
☽ // ☿	1:48
☽ ⚻ ♇	5:04
☽ – ♊	7:34
☽ ✶ ♂	9:31

Today is new Moon day. It is exact at 12:27 this afternoon. Remember that what you start at new Moon tends to bring results at the next full Moon. Obviously it pays to start things that you would like to see the results of and to not start things that you wouldn't. This particular new to full period is more positive than others that we have seen. Be careful with relationships and focus on self-improvement. Today's early through mid predawn is mixed. An innovative approach will work best, but you will want to watch for hard attitudes and exaggerated emotional responses. There may be spaciness in the early morning and a brief period of relationship issues in the late morning. Get anything important done before 12:27 this afternoon as the Moon will be

Astro-Weather

May 2007   Pacific Time

void of course from then until 7:34 tonight when it enters Gemini. At that point the energy will lift noticeably and general moods will tend to become more communicative. Better moods will roll in following the void of course.

Thursday, 17th

☽	∥	♀	1:49
☽	⊻	♀	12:19PM
☽	☌	☿	4:30
☽	☍	♃	11:24

Today's predawn is more open than not and predawners should think in terms of new starts in relationships. The morning is open. Good moods should run through the afternoon. Again, pay attention to relationships. Take a communicative approach from the late afternoon through the evening.

Friday, 18th

☽	□	♅	1:00
☽	⚹	♄	2:09
☽	△	♆	7:20
☽	⊻	☉	4:41PM
☽	☍	♇	5:57
♄	#	♇	6:21
☽	–	♋	8:39

There is a long range outer planet aspect running through the day that will stimulate the image of and expressions reminiscent of 9/11. This is a brief reprise of the dominant energy that animated the original attack. The news should be interesting. Today's early predawn may have a brief period of erratic irritability. This will pass quickly and the rest of the predawn through early morning should be good mood oriented. Most of the rest of the day is open with good moods returning in the late afternoon. There may be a downturn following and you will want to be aware that the Moon will be void of course from 5:57 this afternoon until 8:39 tonight when it enters Cancer. At that point the energy will lift and general moods till tend to become more sensitive and protective. Friday night social scenes will take off as the void of course ends.

Saturday, 19th

☽	□	♂	1:27
☽	∠	♄	3:15
☽	⚼	♆	8:33
☉	⊼	♇	11:05
☽	☌	♀	6:31PM
☽	∠	☉	8:08
☿	☍	♃	10:31

There are two major energies running throughout today. The first easily brings about the unexpected exposure of things normally kept secret and hidden. Keep the eyes and ears open. This energy also brings challenges with and for authority. Stay out of the crossfire. The second indicates an excess of activity involving communication and transportation. Be reasonable. Don't bite off more than you can chew or make undeliverable promises. Watch the early through mid predawn for irritability, aggressiveness and hard attitudes. There may be some spaciness in the mid morning, but this will pass quickly. Pay attention to relationships through the evening, but watch for some minor irritability. This will be a high energy Saturday night, but you will want to deal carefully with it.

Sunday, 20th

☽	⚻	♃	1:43
☽	⚺	☿	2:12
☽	△	♅	3:56
☽	⚺	♄	5:15
☽	//	♀	10:33
☽	⚻	♆	10:40
☽	//	☿	1:24PM
♂	⚼	♄	1:41
☿	□	♅	4:26
☽	⚻	♇	10:00

High energy from yesterday will tend to remain with us through today. It is joined by two more major cautionary energies. The first easily brings about feelings of restriction and frustration and the temptation to act out on it. This is not likely to be a good idea. Consequences from running afoul of this aspect can be harsher and longer lasting than usual. The second brings problems to communication and transportation, especially where electricity, technology, and electronic media are involved. This energy also brings out the nutcases. Watch for erratic and bizarre behavior of all kinds and be especially careful in traffic. Aside from the major energies, moods should be positive through the pre-dawn. Watch the late morning for a brief period of erratic spaciness. Take a communicative approach through the rest of the afternoon. The evening is open.

Monday, 21st

☽	⚹	☉	12:47
☽	–	♌	12:57
☉	–	♊	3:11
☿	⚹	♄	3:48
☽	⚼	♃	4:16
☽	⚼	♅	6:52
☽	∠	☿	8:57
☽	△	♂	9:23
☽	#	♃	9:34
☿	//	♀	5:34PM
☽	//	☉	7:38

Continue to observe yesterday's cautions throughout today. Be aware of a short Moon void of course period this morning from 12:47 to 12:57 when the Moon enters Leo. At that point the energy will lift and general moods will tend to become more intense and concerned with self. The Sun enters the mutable sun sign Gemini early this morning and the final third of the Spring season begins. Pay attention to the details of the major projects begun back at the Vernal Equinox. There are two more major energies running through the day. The first, which will be very welcome, is very positive for matters involving communication and transportation. Solidify projects. This energy is also great for negotiation and coming to long-term agreement. The second works well for communication and new beginnings in relationships. Make a positive gesture. Aside from the major energies the late predawn to mid morning has scattered minor irritability. Moods will improve through the late morning, and the rest of the day and evening is open.

Tuesday, 22nd

☽	⚼	♇	1:33
☽	⚺	♀	5:30
☽	△	♃	7:53
☽	⚻	♅	10:54
☽	☌	♄	12:27PM
☽	⚼	♂	3:13
☽	#	♇	3:29
☽	//	♄	3:48

Continue to make use of yesterday's major energies through today. There is another major energy coming into focus that is very positive for any prayer, meditation, or spiritual practices one may be involved in. Be open to the intuitive process and follow guidance as it is received. Watch the early predawn for a brief period of minor coerciveness. Good moods will run through much of the morning; take an expansive approach. The late morning to midday may have

☽	⚹	☿	5:04
☽	☍	♆	6:02

some minor erratic emotional reactions, but this will pass quickly. The mid to late afternoon may also have minor aggressive attitudes and coercion. Take a communicative approach through the evening, but watch for spaciness. Make good choices.

Wednesday, 23rd

☽	#	♆	12:43
☿	△	♆	12:48
☽	△	♇	6:08
♀	⚻	♃	7:16
☽	—	♍	9:27
☽	∠	♀	1:01PM
☽	□	☉	2:03
☽	⚻	♂	10:15

Major energy mentioned yesterday for spiritual pursuits and the intuitive process will remain with us through much of today. There is another major energy that is highly social and fun oriented. Problems set in with this energy as it stimulates erratic behavior and overindulgence. Some people will prove to themselves yet again that it is possible to get too much of a good thing. The Moon will be void of course this morning from 6:08 until 9:27 when it enters Virgo. At that point the energy will lift noticeably and general moods will tend to become more discerning and concerned with detail. Watch the afternoon for a period of relationship issues and intensely bad moods. The evening will open up, but continue to watch the overindulgence energy.

Thursday, 24th

♂	∠	♆	2:18PM
☽	#	♅	4:45
☽	□	♃	5:52
♆	℞		6:09
☽	⚹	♀	9:34
☽	☍	♅	9:45
☽	⚺	♄	11:34
♀	△	♅	11:41

There are two major energies running throughout today that are widely divergent. The first is highly cautionary. Be very careful around water and hot, caustic liquids and gases. This is a potentially explosive energy. It also tends to stimulate a spacy and inebriation fueled violence. Do not let minor disputes escalate. The second is intensely social and fun oriented. Plan some sort of stimulating and unusual activity. Make a thoughtful but unexpected gesture. Aside from the major energies, most of the daytime is open. Watch the late afternoon through early evening for erratic and exaggerated emotional responses. Moods will be mixed but primarily positive in the late night.

Friday, 25th

☽	⚻	♆	5:10
☽	//	♂	8:28
☽	□	☿	12:38PM
☽	□	♇	5:43
☽	—	♎	9:16
♀	⚺	♄	9:37
☽	#	♂	11:02

The high social energy mentioned yesterday will remain with us through today. There is another major energy that is also positive socially and in relationships. This aspect is very good for strengthening and solidifying relationships. Negotiate a new deal honestly and for the benefit of both. Moods should be positive through most of the predawn but watch the late predawn for a brief period of erratic spaciness. Take an active approach through the rest of the morning. There may be some minor irritability through the midday, but this will pass quickly. Most of the rest of the afternoon is open, but watch the late afternoon to early evening for minor coercive irritability. This will be a high energy, social Friday night, but be aware that the Moon will be void of course from 5:43 this afternoon until 9:16 tonight when it enters Libra. At that point the energy will lift noticeably, general moods will tend to become more con-cerned with balance and beauty, and social energy will take off.

Saturday, 26th

☽	∠	♄	6:02
☽	△	☉	7:21
☽	⚻	♆	11:32
☽	∥	♅	2:05PM
☽	☍	♂	2:37

The high social energy mentioned yesterday will tend to linger through today. Make the right choices and keep the glow going. Moods will be mixed in the early morning. Some will fall prey to hard attitudes, but good moods should dominate. There may be some spaciness at the midday. There may also be a brief period of aggressiveness in the mid afternoon, but this will pass quickly if it is noticed at all. The evening into the late night is open. Choose well and enjoy.

Sunday, 27th

☽	✶	♃	5:58
☿	☍	♆	8:14
☽	⚺	♅	10:39
☽	✶	♄	12:41PM
☽	□	♀	4:13
☽	⚻	☉	4:33
☽	△	♆	6:02

There will be a major energy running throughout the day that bears watching. This aspect easily stimulates problems in communication and transportation, especially where people become coercive, attempt to impose their will, or give in to sarcasm and just plain nasty attitudes. It also easily leads to the exposure of things normally kept secret and hidden. Observe and learn. Aside from the major energy, the predawn is open. Good moods should run through the very early morning. The late morning through the midday is mixed. Avoid erratic emotional reactions and take a disciplined approach. Watch the late afternoon for relationship issues and minor irritability, but this will pass and the evening through the late night becomes more positive and open.

Monday, 28th – Memorial Day

☽	✶	♆	6:31
☽	∥	♆	7:37
☽	△	☿	9:16
☽	→	♏	10:10
☽	∠	♃	12:05PM
♀	⚺	♆	12:53
☽	#	♄	4:25
☽	⚻	♅	5:06
☽	∥	♆	5:21
☿	→	♋	5:56

There are two major energies to deal with today. The first easily brings problems to relationships, especially where intoxicants and spaciness are indulged. This energy is highly social but volatile, as misunderstandings easily arise. The second indicates a general shift in communication and transportation toward a more sensitive mode. Aside from the major energy, the predawn is open. Take a cooperative, intuitive, and communicative approach through the early morning. Be aware of a short Moon void of course period this morning from 9:16 until 10:10 when the Moon enters Scorpio. At that point, the energy will lift and general

May 2007   Pacific Time

moods will tend to become more intense. The late afternoon to early evening may have hard attitudes and erratic emotional responses, but this will pass and the rest of the evening and nighttime is open.

Tuesday, 29ᵗʰ

☽	☍	☉	1:33
☽	☍	♂	7:29
☽	∠	♇	12:40PM
☽	⚺	♃	5:55
☽	⚻	☿	6:50
☉	∠	♀	6:51
☽	△	♅	11:14
☽	#	☉	11:24

There is a major energy running throughout the day that spotlights and emphasizes relationships and aesthetics. This may or may not be experienced as positive. Either way, light will be shed and learning will occur. Watch the early predawn for a brief period of erratic irritability. The early morning will have a minor erratic aggressiveness which will pass quickly. The midday may have a short burst of coercive irritability, but this again will be short-lived. Take an expansive approach, making the right choices, and enjoy the evening into the late night.

Wednesday, 30ᵗʰ

☽	∥	♃	12:59
☽	□	♄	1:27
☽	□	♆	6:20
☽	△	♀	10:10
☽	#	♀	2:10PM
☽	⚻	♂	3:21
☽	⚺	♆	6:25
☽	—	♐	10:06

You will notice energy levels rising throughout today as tomorrow's full Moon takes shape. Consider today to be part of the full Moon period. Today's predawn will start out with good moods but watch for a downturn with hard attitudes. The early morning will have a brief period of spaciness, but this should pass quickly. Most of the rest of the morning has more positive moods. Get anything important done before 10:10 this morning as the Moon will be void of course from then until 10:06 tonight when it enters Sagittarius. At that point the energy will lift noticeably and general moods will tend to become more expansive and open to a wide range of ideas. As the void of course ends, the full Moon kicks in for real.

Thursday, 31ˢᵗ

☽	#	☿	1:54
☽	☍	☿	3:34
☉	#	♃	1:52PM
☽	☌	☉	6:03
☽	⚻	♀	6:17
☽	△	♂	10:37

This is full Moon day. It is exact at 6:03 this evening. Remember that full Moons are always high energy and deserve to be approached with respect. This particular full Moon is more positive than many we have seen. There is another major energy which tends to stimulate feelings of positivity and well-being. The only problem with this energy is that some people tend to get carried away with themselves and ego battles may result. Make good choices and have fun with the high energy.

Pacific Time   June 2007

June 2007

Overview

June will continue the high stakes play at the international level that we saw through May. It will likely be quite the spectacle. At the beginning of June, Jupiter is still in orb of the complex of outer planet aspects making things so crazy, and keeping it all more positive than it would be without it. But it will be fading and by the end of the month will not be of much more help. This leaves us with the last peak of the Saturn opposed Neptune to get through, which will be the last great hurrah in this context for religious conservatives of all kinds who will be making what hay they can with it. This will be the last of this aspect in this cycle, and on the subconscious level, those using it to their ends will know that it's now or never. Watch for all manner of attacks, both successful and failed, and be sure that this will not be a slow news month. The funny thing, and at this point there may not be much laughter going on, is that it peaks late this month and early next, but by the end of next month, Saturn will be back to the trine to Pluto which brought the relative calm to the end of last year. This month may be the dark before the dawn. If enough light has been generated, there will be a fizzling out of hostilities; if not enough light, then suffering will be much greater.

On the more personal level, there will be a period of rough days coming off of late last month's full Moon, especially during the first weekend and a few days following. The 10th through the 13th turns around and becomes much more positive. Make the most of this period. We have mostly garden variety positive and cautionary energies through the rest of the month, but they warrant a glance ahead just the same. You will want to be aware that Mercury turns retrograde on the 15th and backs up through July 9th. See the Retrograde pages at the beginning of this book for more on these periods. There are no all day Moon void of course periods this month, but there are a few half day voids to work around.

Friday, 1st

☽ ☌ ♃   4:18
☽ □ ♅   10:07
☽ △ ♄   12:30PM
☽ ✶ ♆   4:54

Consider the full Moon to remain with us through today and well into tomorrow at least. There is another major energy coming into focus today that can bring problems to communication and transportation. Watch for people running into restrictions and frustration and not responding well to them. Most of today's predawn is open. Take an expansive approach through the late predawn. There may be a brief period of erratic irritability in the late morning, but this will pass quickly and the rest of the afternoon will be more positive. Take a disciplined approach. The late afternoon has good moods as well, and the rest of the evening into the late night is open. Have fun tonight, but remember the caution.

Saturday, 2nd

☽	⚼	♀	1:44
☿	⊿	♄	1:58
☽	☌	♇	4:28
☽	–	♑	8:08
☽	⚻	♄	5:17PM
☽	☍	☿	6:26
☽	⊿	♆	9:25

The cautionary energy mentioned yesterday will tend to remain with us through today. Reread and apply. Watch the mid to late predawn for erratic relationship issues. Be aware that the Moon will be void of course this morning from 4:28 until 8:08 when it enters Capricorn. At that point the energy will lift and general moods will tend to become more down to earth and concerned with accomplishment. Most of the rest of the daytime is open, but watch the late afternoon and early evening for some hard attitudes and argumentativeness. The late night will also have a brief period of spaciness. Enjoy your Saturday night, but make good choices.

Sunday, 3rd

☽	⚼	☉	8:04
☽	□	♂	11:23
♀	⚼	♇	11:23
☽	⚺	♃	12:46PM
☽	✶	♅	7:02
☽	⚼	♄	9:35

There is a major energy running throughout the day that is significantly cautionary. This energy brings about a heavy and potentially coercive sexuality that can pop up unexpectedly and seemingly out of nowhere. While this can be fun for some, it can be unsettling and even dangerous for others. Protect the vulnerable. Aside from the major energy, the predawn is open. The mid through late morning will have periods of erratic irritability and aggressiveness. Once past that, moods will improve through the afternoon and early evening. Watch the later evening for some potential erratic hard attitudes.

Monday, 4th

☽	⚺	♆	1:28
☽	#	☿	7:09
♂	△	♃	7:57
☽	⚺	♇	12:35PM
☿	□	♆	2:04
☽	□	☉	2:10
☽	☍	♀	2:42
☽	–	♒	4:15
☽	⊿	♃	4:19
☽	#	♀	8:07
☽	#	☉	9:32

There are two major energies running through today. The first is high positive energy, pure and simple. This is energy for any sort of activity or project one may be involved in. Some will be tempted to use it for fun and turn today into a three-day weekend. It will work for that, but it's probably best to use this for more important endeavors. The second can bring problems to communication and transportation, especially where inebriants and the otherwise out of it are involved. Watch for a general spaciness and be especially careful in traffic. Aside from the major energies, good moods should run through the predawn. The early morning

Pacific Time   June 2007

| ☽ ⚹ ♅ | 10:45 |

may have a brief period of irritability, but this will pass quickly. Good moods should run from the mid morning through the midday. There may be a downturn in the early to mid afternoon, however, with minor irritability and relationship issues. Be aware that the Moon will be void of course from 2:42 this afternoon until 4:15 when it enters Aquarius. At that point the energy will lift and general moods will tend to become more independent and free-thinking.

Tuesday, 5th

☽ ∥ ♃	1:08
☽ ⊼ ☿	6:01
♀ □ ♃	9:39
♀ → ♌	10:59
☉ ∥ ♀	12:43PM
☽ ⚹ ♇	3:56
☉ ☍ ♃	4:12
☽ ⚹ ♃	7:22
☽ △ ☉	7:39
☽ ⚹ ♂	9:50

There are four major energies to deal with today. The first is highly social and fun-oriented. The problem with this energy is it easily leads to overindulgence. Enjoy it, but don't get carried away. The second indicates a general shift in relationships and aesthetic values toward a more intense and personal mode. The third sheds light on and is very good for making new beginnings in relationships. Make a positive gesture. The fourth is high positive energy that again easily leads to excess and inflated egos. People will be feeling generally positive and good about themselves, but it's very easy to go overboard. Aside from the major energies, take an expansive approach through the predawn. There may be some minor irritability in the very early morning, but this is not likely to amount to much. Most of the rest of the daytime is open. Watch the mid afternoon for a brief period of coercive emotional reactions, but this again will pass quickly if it is noticed at all. Very good moods should run through the later evening and late night.

Wednesday, 6th

☽ ⚹ ♅	2:00
☽ ☍ ♄	4:43
☽ ∥ ♆	5:14
☽ # ♄	6:55
☽ ☌ ♆	8:08
☽ □ ☿	10:37
☽ ∥ ♆	1:43PM
♂ # ♅	5:57
☽ ⚹ ♇	6:46
☽ → ♓	10:23

High energy from yesterday will remain with us through today. Take advantage of the positives and sidestep the cautions. There is another major aspect running through today that is of the more cautionary persuasion. Be on the lookout for sudden, irrational violence, freak accidents, and electrical fires. On higher octaves, this energy can be very good for any activity involving the uses of energy, power, technology, and magic. The right choices need to be made, however, to deal with this energy successfully. Take an innovative approach to the predawn, but watch the late predawn through late morning for minor hard attitudes and some argumentativeness. Be open to the intuitive process through the afternoon. Moods should be positive in the evening, but be aware that the Moon will be void of course tonight from 6:46 until 10:23 when it enters Pisces. At that

Astro-Weather

June 2007   Pacific Time

point the energy will lift and general moods will tend to become more mellow, if a bit spacy.

Thursday, 7th

☽	⚻	♀	1:07
☽	∠	♂	2:09
☽	△	☿	2:27PM

Today's early predawn may have a period of erratic relationship issues followed by tantrums and aggressive attitudes. Once past that, the morning through most of the afternoon is open. Take a communicative approach through the afternoon. The evening into the late night is open.

Friday, 8th

☽	□	♃	12:00
☽	#	♂	12:36
☽	//	♅	1:58
☽	□	☉	4:42
☽	⚻	♀	5:20
☽	⚺	♂	5:51
☽	☌	♅	6:54
♀	#	♃	7:43
☽	⚻	♄	9:45
☽	⚺	♆	12:43PM
☽	□	♇	10:51

There are three major energies to deal with today. The first is a reprise of the high social energy from a few days ago. It's Friday, go ahead and have some fun with this energy, but do guard against overindulgence. You will see people proving yet again that it is possible to get too much of a good thing. The second is positive for any activity involving energy, power, technology and magic. There is likely to be much communication along these lines, and a lot may be accomplished. This aspect also works very well for fun and stimulating activities, and of course that is how many will choose to use it. The third is the fly in the ointment that easily leads to problems in relationships. Be on the lookout for sudden, irrational and unreasonable demands for change. Choices are obviously in order. There is scattered minor irritability through the predawn with a period of intensely bad moods in the late predawn to early morning. Watch the mid morning for erratic hard attitudes. Moods will improve through the afternoon and most of the evening. Have fun tonight but remember to choose well and be aware that the Moon will be void of course from 10:51 into tomorrow's predawn.

Saturday, 9th

♂	⚺	♅	1:48
☽	—	♈	2:25
♀	□	♅	4:26
☽	△	♀	8:50
☽	⚻	♄	11:27
☉	□	♅	1:08PM
☽	∠	♆	2:12
☽	#	♅	3:42
☽	//	♂	6:51
☽	□	☿	7:47

Last night's Moon void of course period ends at 2:25 this morning when the Moon enters Aries At that point the energy will lift and general moods will tend to become more assertive and aggressive. The high energy mentioned yesterday will remain very much with us through today. Focus on the fun but be mindful of the cautionary relationship energy. There is another major aspect to deal with today that is definitely cautionary and is in bad combination with the relationship energy. Watch for erratic and bizarre behavior of all kinds as the crazies emerge in full force. This energy also easily brings about problems with and for authority. There will be a great deal of volatility across the board today and good choices will be very important. At higher octaves, all of this can be fun, but not everyone will be able to approach it on those levels. Minor aspects are mixed at best and have I mentioned good choices?

Sunday, 10th

☽	△	♃	2:34
☽	⚺	♅	9:41
☽	⚹	☉	11:07
☽	☌	♂	11:23
☽	△	♄	12:40PM
☽	⚹	♆	3:13
☉	∥	☿	10:48

High energy from the past few days will tend to linger through today. There may be many people dealing with fallout. There are two more major energies coming into focus throughout today. The first is positive for looking within and coming to greater self-understanding. The second is positive for any activity one may be involved in. For those not still embroiled in the recent cautionary energy, this will be a go-for-it day. Minor aspects are predominantly positive and good moods should reign.

Monday, 11th

☽	△	♇	12:56
☽	#	♆	2:10
☽	⚼	♃	3:11
☉	⚹	♂	3:26
☽	→	♉	4:28
☽	∥	♄	7:53
☽	#	♇	10:04
☽	∠	♅	10:26
☉	⚹	♄	12:40PM
☽	∠	☉	1:33
☽	□	♀	2:07
♂	△	♄	3:42
☽	⚹	☿	10:34

High positive energy from yesterday will continue strongly through today and is joined by two more major positive aspects. The first illuminates all things involving authority, discipline, older people, and traditional matters. This energy is also very good for negotiation and coming to long term agreement. This may be the day to deal with the boss about that issue. The second combines with the first and adds power to it. This energy by itself is excellent for any activity involving the use of energy and power, especially in the pursuit of building or forming things. Efforts along these lines can produce results beyond any reasonable expectation. This is the classic go-for-it day. Do be aware that the Moon will be void of course this morning from 12:56 until 4:28 when it enters Taurus. At that point the energy will lift and general moods will tend to become more down to earth and concerned with enjoyment. Minor aspects, unfortunately, do not help the cause and there is scattered minor irritability throughout the daytime. This is likely to pop up mainly in cases of people being in the way of those out to accomplish. Lead, follow, or get out of the way.

Tuesday, 12th

☽	⚼	♇	1:26
☽	⚻	♃	3:30
☽	∥	♀	5:37
☽	⚹	♅	10:55
☽	#	♃	10:57
☽	□	♄	2:06PM
☽	∥	☿	3:07

High positive energy from yesterday will remain with us through today and you will want to make the best possible use of it. It is joined by another major energy that will come into focus as the day wears on that is very positive for any sort of prayer, meditation, or spiritual activity. This energy is also excellent for the intuitive process, and much guidance will be available to those open to it. Pay special

June 2007   **Pacific Time**

☽ ⚺ ♂	3:08
☽ ⚺ ☉	3:42
☽ □ ♆	4:17
☽ ∥ ☉	6:17
☽ ⚼ ☿	11:24

attention to any dreams you may remember. Aside from the major energy, watch the early through mid predawn for minor coerciveness and exaggerated emotional reactions. Pay attention to relationships in the late predawn to early morning and take an innovative, expansive approach through the late morning. The early to mid afternoon may have a brief period of hard attitudes but this will pass quickly to be replaced by much more positive moods that may give way to some spaciness. Be aware that the Moon will be void of course from 4:17 this afternoon through most of tomorrow's predawn.

Wednesday, 13th

☉ △ ♆	12:29
☽ ⚻ ♇	1:48
☽ – ♊	5:23
♂ ✶ ♆	1:35PM
☽ ⚼ ♂	4:51
☽ ✶ ♀	6:16

Last night's Moon void of course period runs through most of today's predawn and ends at 5:23 this morning when the Moon enters Gemini. At that point the energy will lift noticeably and general moods will tend to become more communicative. Positive energy from the past few days remains with us yet through today. There are two more major energies. The first is an addition to and continuation of the positive energy mentioned yesterday. Any sort of spiritual activity will be highly energized. Be very open to the intuitive process and act on the guidance. You will notice energy levels rising through the day as the second major energy, tomorrow's new Moon, rolls in.

Thursday, 14th

☽ ⚺ ☿	12:08
☽ ☍ ♃	3:59
☽ □ ♅	11:56
☽ ✶ ♄	3:25PM
☽ △ ♆	5:18
☽ ✶ ♂	6:49
☽ ☌ ☉	8:13
☽ ⚼ ♀	8:36

Today is new Moon day. It is exact at 8:13 tonight. Remember that what you start at new Moon brings results at the next full Moon. The high positive energy leading up to this new Moon will make for good beginnings. Pay particular attention to relationships, however, and be aware of the Mercury Retrograde starting tomorrow. Aside from the major energies, take a communicative and expansive approach through the predawn. Watch the midday for a brief period of erratic emotional reactions. The rest of the afternoon becomes more positive, and good moods should run from the mid afternoon through much of the evening. There may be minor relationship issues in the late night.

Friday, 15th

☽ ☍ ♇	2:59
☽ – ♋	6:45
☽ ⚼ ♄	4:37PM
☿ ℞	4:41
☿ # ♃	4:45

Consider the new Moon to run through today and much of tomorrow at least. Today's biggest news is that Mercury turns retrograde early this evening and backs up in our sky until July 9th. During a Mercury retrograde, all things having to do with communication and transportation are prone

Pacific Time   June 2007

☽	⚼	♆	6:23
☽	⚼	♀	11:30

to snafu and breakdown. Plan extra time for everything; watch for all manner of misunderstanding; avoid the signing of contracts and legal documents; and don't open new businesses. See the Mercury Retrograde page at the beginning of this book for more on these periods. The Moon will be void of course this morning from 2:59 until 6:45 when it enters Cancer. At that point the energy will lift and general moods will tend to become more sensitive and protective. There is a major energy running through the day that will stimulate a great deal of activity involving communication and transportation. Remember the retrograde.

Saturday, 16th

☽	☌	☿	2:21
☽	⚻	♃	5:45
☽	△	♅	2:32PM
☽	⚼	♄	6:31
☽	⚻	♆	8:09

Good moods should run through today's early predawn. Take a communicative approach through the mid predawn. The late predawn may have a brief period of erratic, exaggerated emotional reactions, but this will pass quickly if it is noticed at all. The morning through midday is open. Good moods will run from the mid afternoon through early evening. Take an innovative yet disciplined and communicative approach. Watch for spaciness in the later evening and this may not be the most positive, social Saturday night on record.

Sunday, 17th

☽	□	♂	12:40
☽	⚼	☉	3:06
☽	⚻	♆	6:19
☽	⚼	♃	7:40
☽	∥	☉	10:43
☽	—	♌	10:26
☿	⚼	♀	4:39PM
☽	⚼	♅	4:59
☽	#	♃	7:39
☽	∥	☿	10:51

The Moon will be void of course this morning from 12:40 until 10:26 when it enters Leo. At that point the energy will lift noticeably and general moods will tend to become more intense and concerned with self. Relax and take it easy through the void of course and be prepared for the rush of energy as it ends. There is a major energy running throughout the day that would normally be very good for communication in relationships. Remember, however, that Mercury is retrograde and issues from the past are likely to pop up. Try to use this energy for healing old wounds. Minor aspects are of little help through the day and good choices will be needed.

Monday, 18th

☽	⚼	☿	6:53
☉	∠	♀	7:52
☽	∠	☉	8:07
☽	☌	♀	8:07
☽	⚼	♆	9:18
☽	△	♃	10:30
☽	∥	♀	10:47

There are three major energies running throughout today. The first sheds light on relationships, but it may be a harsh light and you will want to manage your reactions to things well. The second also sheds light, but on things normally kept secret and hidden. Guard your secrets and keep the eyes and ears open as there will be much to learn. This energy also stimulates challenges with and for authority.

Astro-Weather

June 2007 Pacific Time

☽	⚻	♅	8:25PM
☽	#	♇	11:01
☉	☍	♇	11:49

Regime change will be in the air on many levels. This is not the day to mess with the boss or other authority figures, and be careful not to get caught in anyone else's crossfire. The third easily brings about a heavy and potentially coercive sexuality. As always with this energy, protect the vulnerable. Minor aspects are mixed, with the best moods occurring in the very early morning and in the late morning. Choose well at all other times.

Tuesday, 19th

☽	☌	♄	1:04
♀	□	♇	1:16
☽	☍	♆	2:22
☽	∥	♄	2:33
☽	#	♆	7:54
☽	⚼	☿	10:20
☽	△	♂	10:38
☽	△	♇	1:15PM
☽	✶	☉	2:22
♀	△	♃	3:48
☽	—	♍	5:45

The high cautionary energy mentioned yesterday will continue through today. Reread the cautions and apply carefully, especially the one concerning the heavy and potentially coercive sexuality. There is another major energy running throughout the day that is much more positive. This is party energy pure and simple that is really much more appropriate to a weekend than the middle of the work week. It may not be easy for many people to focus on work related activities and smart management might want to schedule some kind of play day. Aside from the major energies, you will want to take a disciplined approach through the predawn and watch for spaciness. The early through late morning may also have some spaciness and argumentativeness as well. Moods will improve markedly through the rest of the afternoon, but do be aware that the Moon will be void of course this afternoon from 2:22 until 5:45 when it enters Virgo. At that point the energy will lift and general moods will tend to become more discerning and concerned with detail. Have fun tonight, but try not to get too carried away.

Wednesday, 20th

☽	∥	♂	8:02
☽	✶	☿	2:30PM
☽	□	♂	5:20
☽	□	♃	7:00
☽	⚼	♀	9:20

The high social energy mentioned yesterday will tend to remain with us through today. Try to get some work done. Today's predawn is open. Take an active approach through the morning. A communicative attitude will serve best through most of the afternoon. There may be some minor aggressiveness in the late afternoon to early evening, followed by a tendency towards exaggerated emotional reaction, but neither of these energies should amount to very much. Moods will improve later.

Thursday, 21st

☽	#	♅	12:03
☽	☍	♅	6:09
♂	△	♆	6:36
☉	—	♋	11:06

There are three major energies running throughout the day. The first is very positive for the use of energy and power for deep transformation. Make those important changes you have been contemplating. The second is the Sun's entry into

☽	⚺	♄	11:32
☽	⚻	♆	12:24PM
♂	⚼	♃	5:42
☽	□	♇	11:50

the cardinal water sign Cancer late this morning. This is the Summer Solstice. At this point we should conduct an examination of our major projects begun back at the Vernal Equinox to see how they should be adjusted and otherwise nurtured. The third is related to the first and serves to enlarge the energy. Watch for some people to get carried away. In extreme cases conflict can result. Make good choices to get the most out of this day but be aware that the Moon will be void of course from 11:50 tonight well into tomorrow's predawn.

Friday, 22nd

☽	⚻	♂	1:00
☽	–	♎	4:43
☽	∠	♀	5:24
☽	□	☉	6:15
☽	∠	♄	5:51PM
☽	⚼	♆	6:27
☽	//	♅	8:02

Last night's Moon void of course period ends at 4:43 this morning when it enters Libra. At that point the energy will lift and general moods will tend to become more concerned with balance and beauty. High energy from the past two days will tend to linger through today. Reread. There may be minor relationship issues following the void of course and a period of very bad moods follows that. Things will lighten up by the late morning and most of the afternoon is open. Watch the late afternoon through early evening for hard attitudes and spaciness. This may not be the most positive social Friday night that you've ever experienced and good choices will be needed.

Saturday, 23rd

☽	□	☿	12:22
☽	⚹	♃	6:27
♅	℞		7:43
☽	⚹	♀	2:00PM
☽	#	♂	4:35
☽	⚻	♅	6:31

Watch the early predawn for a brief period of irritability and argumentativeness. The rest of the predawn is open. Good moods should run through the morning and much of the afternoon. There may be some aggressive attitudes in the late afternoon followed by a short burst of erratic irritability in the early evening, but both of these may well pass largely unnoticed. Moods will improve in the late night and get better the later it gets. Have fun, but choose well.

Sunday, 24th

☽	⚹	♄	12:30
☽	△	♆	12:48
☽	⚹	♇	12:22PM
☽	∠	♃	12:34
☽	//	♆	2:24
♂	–	♉	2:26
☽	–	♏	5:26
☽	☍	♂	5:38
☽	#	♄	7:08
☽	//	♇	11:55

There is a major energy today that indicates a general shift in the way energy and power are used toward a more down-to-earth mode. Late Saturday night social scenes will remain positively energized well into today's predawn. The morning is open. Moods will be good into the afternoon, but be aware that the Moon will be void of course this afternoon from 12:22 until 5:26 when it enters Scorpio. At that point the energy will lift noticeably and general moods will tend to become more intense. Watch the late afternoon to early evening following the void of course for a period of aggres-

June 2007   Pacific Time

siveness. There may also be some hard attitudes an hour or so after that. Neither of these should amount to much and good choices should handle them easily.

Monday, 25th

☽	△	☉	12:16
☽	⛎	♅	12:53
☽	#	♀	1:38
♄	☍	♆	8:53
☽	△	☿	10:32
☽	#	♃	3:57PM
☽	⚻	♃	6:33
☽	∠	♇	6:33

There are two major energies running throughout the day. The first is a long range outer planet aspect that fuels the flames of the ongoing international as well as domestic political conflict. It's not likely to bring peace any closer to the two sides on the American political scene either. Watch the news. The second easily brings about a heavy and potentially coercive sexuality. While this can be fun for some it can be unsettling and even dangerous for others. As always with this energy, protect the vulnerable. Good moods should dominate the predawn, but irritability will be available for those who insist on it. The morning early afternoon is open. Watch the mid afternoon for a brief period of irritability. The later evening is mixed. Choose well.

Tuesday, 26th

♀	#	♆	1:25
☽	∥	♃	5:12
☽	□	♀	6:52
☽	△	♅	7:00
♀	⚻	♅	8:44
☽	⛎	☉	8:58
☽	□	♆	1:06PM
☽	□	♄	1:22
☽	⛎	☿	3:09
☽	#	☉	4:32

The cautionary relationship energy mentioned yesterday involving the heavy and potentially coercive sexuality will remain with us through today. Continue to protect the vulnerable. It is joined by another major energy that also easily brings problems to relationships. Watch for sudden unrealistic and unreasonable demands for change. As soon as erratic behavior shows up, you will want to switch to damage control. This energy is also highly social and many will use it that way, but it is tricky at that level as well and you will want to be careful in any social situation you find yourself. Aside from a period of good moods in the early morning, there is scattered irritability throughout the day. Get anything important done before 1:22 this afternoon as the Moon will be void of course from then through most of tomorrow's predawn. Relax and take it easy through the nighttime.

Wednesday, 27th

☽	⚻	♇	12:19
☽	→	♐	5:23
☽	⚹	♂	9:20
☽	⚹	☉	5:03PM
☽	⚹	☿	7:16
☿	∠	♄	10:09

Yesterday's Moon void of course period runs through most of today's predawn and ends at 5:23 this morning when the Moon enters Sagittarius. At that point the energy will lift noticeably and general moods will tend to become more expansive and open to a wide range of ideas. High energy from the past two days will tend to linger through today, if only as fallout. There is another major energy running through the day that can bring problems to communication

☽	☌	♃	5:08
☿	□	♆	10:31
☉	☌	☿	11:39
☉	□	♆	12:19PM
☽	□	♂	4:11
☽	□	♅	5:36
☽	△	♀	9:17
☉	∠	♄	10:41
☽	✶	♆	11:23

☽	△	♄	12:12
♀	∥	♄	6:00
☽	☌	♇	10:06
☿	∠	♀	12:34PM
☽	—	♑	3:04
♂	∠	♅	4:42
☽	△	♂	10:16

☽	☍	☿	1:52
☽	□	♀	3:18

and transportation, especially where people run into restriction and frustration and act out on it. Watch for problems from the past to recur. Minor aspects are of no help and this is a day for good choices.

Thursday, 28th

Cautionary energy involving communication and transportation mentioned yesterday will remain with us through today. It is joined by four more major energies. The first adds spaciness to the mix, and if you meet someone who seems a nugget short of a Happy Meal, they likely are. The second can be good for looking within and coming to deeper self-understanding. Again, lessons from the past may be learned. The third adds to the spaciness mentioned above and also easily brings about problems with and for authority. The fourth adds to the third an element of restriction and frustration that can lead to harsh consequences for those unable to resist acting out. Minor aspects are again of little help, but good moods should roll in through the very late night.

Friday, 29th

Be aware that the Moon will be void of course from 10:06 this morning until 3:04 this afternoon when it enters Capricorn. At that point the energy will lift and general moods will tend to become more down to earth and concerned with accomplishment. All the high cautionary energy mentioned yesterday will be with us through today and is joined by four major energies. The first can be positive for making new beginnings in and strengthening and solidifying relationships. This will have to be handled carefully, however, in light of the other energies active at this time. The second can bring about problems in relationships, especially where old disputes are allowed to reignite. Comparisons should not even be thought about much less talked about. Let sleeping dogs lie. The third is the most cautionary of the lot. Watch for sudden unexpected violence, freak accidents and electrical fires. Do not let minor disputes escalate and back away from anyone behaving bizarrely out in the world. You will notice energy levels rising through the day as tomorrow morning's full Moon rolls in. Consider tonight to be full Moon. This will be a very active Friday night, but one to be careful with.

Saturday, 30th

Today is full Moon day. It is exact at 6:48 this morning. Remember that full Moons are always high energy and deserve

June 2007   Pacific Time

☽ ∠ ♆   3:36
☽ ⛛ ♄   4:40
☽ ☍ ☉   6:48
♀ ☍ ♆   8:31
☽ ⚺ ♃   1:22PM

to be approached with caution. This particular full Moon is surrounded by cautionary energies and you will want to be especially careful in social situations and in dealing with relationships. There is another major energy running through today that is very highly social but also very spacy. Be especially careful where recreational substances are indulged and watch for the otherwise out of it. Aside from the major energies, today's predawn should start out with good moods, but watch for a downturn in the mid predawn. Moods will improve in the afternoon and the evening is open. Have fun tonight, but be mindful of the cautions and the full Moon.

July 2007

Overview

As July opens, we are still in the throes of the last peak of the Saturn opposed Neptune. This is the Grade A, number one prime energy for religious conservatism of any kind. There will be a desperation in attempts to whip up the various flocks to action. Watch especially the last week or so of the month as Mars gets involved and what got started earlier in the month comes to a head. As the month progresses, however, Saturn will move away from the opposition to Neptune and toward a trine to Pluto. This is very good news as this is the energy that will eventually bring the end to this round of international lunacy that came to broad public attention on 9/11 of 2001. This energy will build through this month and peak the next. This is not the end, but it is a serious signal of the end. When it returns through the spring of next year, all but the most recalcitrant of belligerents will be facing the writing on the wall. The people of the world will have had enough, at least for this round. Things will likely be much quieter later in the month. Cleanup from the past few months should be the dominant focus, although there may still be some holdout hostilities active. There may be no better time than now to enlist more people in large scale prayer and meditation for peace efforts. It's likely that they've seen enough of the opposite.

On more personal levels, July will tend to be a more normal month than what we've had recently, at least for those not caught up in the above energies. Except that Mercury will be retrograde until the 9th and then take several days to get back up to speed. And then we have Venus turning retrograde on the 27th and backing up in our skies until September 8th. See the Retrograde pages at the beginning of this book for more on these periods. Do be especially careful during the last week and especially the last few days of the month. Read ahead and plan for dealing with all the high energies. The most significant daytime Moon void of course periods are on the 1st, 14th and 24th. There are a few half day voids to work around as well.

Sunday, 1st

☽	⚹	♅	1:44
☽	⚺	♆	7:15
♀	☌	♄	7:39
☽	⚻	♄	8:32
☽	⚻	♀	8:35

Consider the full Moon to run through today and much of tomorrow at least. There are three major energies running through today. The first would normally be positive for making new beginnings in and solidifying relationships. With the attending energies, you will want to deal carefully

July 2007   *Pacific Time*

with this. Make a positive gesture, but keep your expectations reasonable. The second is positive for any activity involving communication and transportation. Remember, however, that Mercury is retrograde and things may not go as swimmingly as we would hope. It is probably best to use this energy for cleaning up old business. The third brings more spaciness to relationships, as if we required any more of it. If all of this is not enough, the Moon will be void of course from 1:44 this morning until 10:23 tonight when it enters Aquarius. At that point the energy will lift noticeably and general moods will tend to become more independent and free thinking. Relax, lay low, and enjoy the day as best you can.

Monday, 2nd

Today we get a bit of a respite from the high energy, but you will want to watch for fallout from the past few days. There may be a brief period of minor irritability in the early predawn, but this is likely to pass unnoticed. Most of the rest of the predawn is open. Watch the late predawn through early morning for erratic emotional responses and argumentativeness. Take an expansive approach in the early to mid morning but watch for aggressiveness and pushy attitudes. Most of the afternoon opens up, but the late afternoon may have another brief period of erratic emotional reactions. Moods will be mixed in the evening. Good choices will yield good moods, but some people will fall prey to irritability and coercive attitudes.

Tuesday, 3rd

There is a major energy running throughout today that has that old good news/bad news thing. People will be feeling generally positive, self-confident, and good about themselves. The bad news is that it is very easy to get carried away with this energy and ego battles may result. Be careful in any dealings with authority. Don't let initial warmth lead you to presume a familiarity that may not be appreciated or tolerated. This energy also easily leads to all manner of overindulgence and people will once again be proving to themselves that it is possible to get too much of a good thing. Aside from the major energy, today's predawn may start out with a brief period of irritability, but this will pass quickly and the rest of the predawn is open. Good moods should run through the early morning, but watch the mid morning for more minor irritability. Take an intuitive, disciplined approach to the afternoon, but watch for hard attitudes. Be on the lookout for relationship issues from the late afternoon through the evening. Choices. Also be aware that the Moon will be void of course from 11:01 tonight well into tomorrow's predawn.

Wednesday, 4th – Independence Day

Last night's Moon void of course period ends at 3:51 this morning when the Moon enters Pisces. At that point the energy will lift and general moods will tend to become more mellow if a bit spacy. Relax and take it easy through the void of course. Most of the morning is open, with good moods through the late morning. Most of the afternoon is open again, followed by good moods in the late afternoon. The nighttime is open to do with as you will and this should be a fun and enjoyable day for most of us.

Thursday, 5th

There may be a brief period of exaggerated emotional responses in the early predawn. Very good moods will roll through the mid predawn. Take an innovative approach through the morning. Good moods should run through the early evening. Take a fun approach and be open to the intuitive process. There will be a downturn in the evening with hard attitudes, irritability and relationship issues. Good choices will be needed to keep the earlier glow going.

Friday, 6th

There is a major energy running through the day that can be positive for making new beginnings in relationships, especially the male/female variety. Watch today's early predawn however for irritability and relationship issues. The mid predawn will have a brief period of coercive irritability. The Moon will be void of course this morning from 3:08 until 7:56 when it enters Aries. At that point the energy will lift noticeably and general moods will tend to become more assertive and aggressive. The morning following the void of course is open. Watch the midday for a brief period of irritability and argumentativeness. The rest of the afternoon to the early evening is open, but there is scattered minor irritability through the rest of the evening into the late night. Have fun tonight but choose well.

Saturday, 7th

Moods will improve in today's early predawn. The mid predawn is mixed. Take an expansive, friendly and fun approach, but watch for potential minor relationship issues.

☽	⚺	♅	3:39PM
☽	⚹	♆	8:37
☽	△	♄	11:14
☽	//	♀	11:21

The early morning is open, but watch the mid morning into the midday for a period of intensely bad moods. Once past that, good moods return and will run from the mid afternoon through the late night. Good choices will lead to a fun and enjoyable day. Bad choices ...

Sunday, 8th

☽	//	♂	3:29
☽	⚼	♃	4:33
☽	△	♀	5:34
☽	△	♇	6:05
☽	#	♆	8:20
☽	//	♄	10:01
☽	–	♉	10:53
☽	⚹	☿	3:09PM
☽	#	♇	3:56
☽	∠	♅	4:57
♀	△	♇	6:09

There is a major energy running throughout today that can be very positive for taking relationships to deeper levels. There is a rather intensely sexual component to this, however, that not everyone is comfortable with. Have fun, but be sensitive to the needs and boundaries of others. Good moods should run through today's predawn. The Moon will be void of course this morning from 6:05 until 10:53 when it enters Taurus. At that point the energy will lift noticeably and general moods will tend to become more down to earth and concerned with enjoyment. The early afternoon is open. Take a communicative approach through the mid to late afternoon, but watch for coercive irritability. There may be some minor erratic emotional reactions, but this, again, will pass quickly. The rest of the night time is open. Make good choices and enjoy this day.

Monday, 9th

☽	//	☿	2:53
☽	☌	♂	4:25
☽	⚻	♃	5:37
☽	⚼	♇	7:15
☽	#	♃	3:39PM
☽	⚹	☉	4:00
☽	∠	☿	4:12
☽	⚹	♅	6:04
☿	D		7:16
☽	//	☉	7:56
☽	□	♆	10:57

Mercury turns direct later this evening after having backed up in our sky since the evening of June 15th. Over the next several days as Mercury picks up speed, the unusually high number of incidents of problems involving communication and transportation that we've had over the last three weeks will fade out. There's another major energy coming into focus throughout the day that is of the cautionary persuasion. There will be a tremendous amount of energy available, but it will be difficult to contain and put to positive use. Watch for people getting carried away, biting off more than they can chew, and making bigger promises than they should. It will be easy to find yourself in these places before you know you've gone there. Minor aspects are mixed throughout the day and good choices will be very important.

Tuesday, 10th

☽	□	♄	2:00
♂	⚻	♃	2:24
☽	⚻	♇	8:18
☽	□	♀	9:53
☽	–	♊	1:09PM
☽	⚺	☿	5:21

The high cautionary energy mentioned yesterday will remain very much with us today. Reread and apply. There is another major energy running through today that is very positive. This aspect is excellent for any activity involving self-discipline, authority, technology, and magic. Be open to innovation and positive change in unusual ways. In the

Pacific Time   July 2007

| ☽ | ∠ | ☉ | 6:53 |
| ☉ | △ | ⚷ | 10:32 |

background, however, there is another major energy that will be more active tomorrow and easily leads to secret and coercive activities. Go for it today because of the positive energy, but do keep an eye on motives, yours and others. Work around the Moon void of course period that runs from 9:53 this morning until 1:09 this afternoon when the Moon enters Gemini. At that point the energy will lift noticeably and general moods will tend to become more communicative. Minor aspects are mixed at best through today, so choose well.

Wednesday, 11th

☽	☍	♃	7:33
☽	⚼	♂	9:14
♂	⚻	♇	12:22PM
☽	□	⚷	8:17
☽	⚼	☉	9:52

All the high energy mentioned yesterday will remain with us through today. Try to make good use of the positive. There is a major energy that is exact this afternoon that is of the cautionary persuasion. Watch for secret and coercive activities of all kinds which, in extreme cases, can extend all the way to violence. Do not let minor disputes escalate and under no circumstances allow yourself to be drawn into altercations with strangers. Motives. Aside from the major energies, the predawn is open. The early morning may have some exaggerated emotional responses, but good moods should win out through the daytime. Most of the evening is open, but the later evening is mixed. Choose well.

Thursday, 12th

☽	△	♆	1:11
☽	⚹	♄	4:44
☽	☍	♇	10:39
☽	∠	♂	11:51
☽	⚹	♀	2:12PM
☽	—	♋	3:39
☽	☌	☿	8:34

Continue to observe yesterday's cautions through today. Reread and apply. Aside from the major energy, good moods should run through the predawn and much of the morning. Watch the late morning through midday for coercive attitudes and aggressiveness. Good moods will return through the rest of the afternoon, but be aware of a short Moon void of course period from 2:12 until 3:39 when the Moon enters Cancer. At that point the energy will lift and general moods will tend to become more sensitive and protective. Take a communicative approach through night time.

Friday, 13th

☽	⚻	♆	2:39
☽	∠	♄	6:30
☽	⚻	♃	10:12
☽	⚹	♂	2:53PM
♂	#	♆	4:37
☽	∠	♀	4:48
☉	⚻	♆	10:10
☽	△	⚷	11:32

There are three major energies to deal with today. The first two will bring out the space cases in a major way. The first easily leads to a potential spacy violence. Be very careful around water and hot and caustic liquids and gases. This is an explosive energy. The second brings about general spaciness and can stimulate problems with and for authority. This will be a day to keep your head down and avoid coming to the attention of bosses and others in power. Watch for the inebriated and otherwise out of it and be especially careful in traffic. You will notice energy levels rising throughout the day as the third energy, tomorrow morning's new Moon rolls in. Have fun tonight, but be mindful of the cautions and the new Moon and be good.

Saturday, 14th

☽	⊼	♆	4:34
☽	☌	☉	5:03
☽	⚺	♄	8:48
♂	∥	♄	9:13
♀	–	♍	11:26
☽	⚼	♃	12:12PM
☽	⊼	♇	2:25
☽	–	♌	7:44
☽	⚺	♀	8:00

Today is new Moon day. It is exact at 5:03 this morning. Remember that what you start at new Moon brings results at the next full Moon. This particular new to full Moon period should be handled carefully. Focus on self-discipline. High energies from the past couple of days will tend to remain with us through today. They are joined by two more major energies. The first is very good for new beginnings involving the use of energy, power, and discipline. The second indicates a general shift in relationship energy and aesthetic sensibilities toward a more discerning and detailed mode. Be aware that the Moon will be void of course from 5:03 this morning until 7:44 tonight when it enters Leo. At that point the energy will lift very noticeably and general moods will tend to become more intense and concerned with self. Try to relax and take it easy through the Moon void of course and tend to old business. There will be a huge boost in Saturday night social energy as the void of course ends. Have fun tonight, but remember the new Moon.

Sunday, 15th

☽	□	♅	1:59
☽	⚺	☿	2:19
☽	∥	☉	5:40
☽	#	♃	6:00
☽	∥	☿	2:25PM
☽	△	♃	2:54
☉	#	♃	3:56
☽	□	♇	5:15
☽	□	♂	11:07

Consider the new Moon to remain with us through today and much of tomorrow. Make the new beginnings today that you would have made yesterday if not for the long void of course. There's another major energy running through the day that stimulates feelings of positivity and wellbeing. The only problem with this energy is that people can easily get carried away. In extreme cases ego battles may occur. Overindulgence of all kinds is also associated with this energy. Minor aspects are mixed, but with the right choices this should be a fun and enjoyable day for most of us.

Monday, 16th

☽	⊼	♅	5:10
☽	⚼	☿	6:42
☽	#	♆	7:16
☽	☍	♆	10:30
☽	∥	♂	12:52PM
☽	∥	♄	3:20
☽	⚺	☉	3:25

There is a major energy running throughout the day that is very positive for dealing with self-discipline, authority, older people, and traditional matters. Seek to establish greater stability in your own life and in situations you are involved in. Aside from the major energy, most of today's predawn is open. Watch the late predawn through early morning for erratic emotional responses and coercive irritability. The

☽	#	♆	3:31
☽	☌	♄	3:33
☉	⚺	♄	5:16
☽	△	♇	8:56

late morning contributes spaciness. Take an active and disciplined approach through the afternoon. Good moods should return in the mid afternoon, but watch for lingering spaciness. The evening is open and good moods make another appearance. Do be aware that the Moon will be void of course from 8:56 tonight well into tomorrow's predawn.

Tuesday, 17th

☽	–	♍	2:40
☽	☌	♀	4:40
♄	#	♆	11:53
☽	⚹	☿	12:19PM
☽	//	♀	2:55
☽	∠	☉	10:11
☽	□	♃	10:45

Last night's Moon void of course period runs through most of today's predawn and ends at 2:40 this morning when the Moon enters Virgo. At that point the energy will lift and general moods will tend to become more discerning and concerned with detail. There is a major energy running throughout the day that is long range outer planet aspect that may bring more headlines in the ongoing international conflict as well as in domestic politics. Minor aspects are neutral to positive and with the right choices this can be a good day.

Wednesday, 18th

☉	⚼	♃	5:09
☽	#	♅	7:23
☽	△	♂	11:07
☽	☍	♅	2:06PM
☽	⚻	♆	7:42

There are two major energies to deal with today. The first generates a feeling of general positivity and well-being. People will be feeling confident and good about themselves. The problem with this energy is that it is easy to get carried away with and ego battles can result. Also watch for all manner of overindulgence. The second easily brings problems to communication and transportation, especially where the inebriated and otherwise out of it are involved. Be especially careful in traffic. Aside from the major energies, the predawn is open. Watch the early morning for an erratic irritability, but this will pass quickly. Take an active approach through the late morning. The early to mid afternoon may have another brief bout of erratic emotional reactions. The evening chips in with spaciness. Choose well.

Thursday, 19th

☽	⚺	♄	1:43
☿	⚼	♆	3:00
☽	⚹	☉	5:56
☽	□	♇	6:44
☽	–	♎	12:54PM
☉	⚻	♇	3:47
☽	⚺	♀	4:34
☽	⚼	♂	6:29
☉	//	☿	11:15

There are three major energies to deal with today. The first brings out the space cases. Watch for those overdoing recreational substances and others slipping off their meds. Be extra careful in traffic. The second easily brings about the exposure of things normally kept secret and hidden in sudden and unexpected ways. Guard your secrets and observe as others' are exposed. Stay awake as there may be much to learn. This aspect also brings trouble with and for authority. Don't mess with the boss and don't get caught in anyone else's crossfire. The third is very good for looking within and coming to deeper self understanding. Aside from the major energies, moods should be primarily positive. Be aware of a Moon void of course period running from 6:44 this morning until 12:54 this afternoon when the Moon enters Libra. At that point the energy will lift noticeably and general moods will tend to become more concerned with balance and beauty.

Friday, 20th

Yesterday's cautionary energies for the exposure of secrets and trouble with authority, as well as the positive energy for introspection, will tend to linger through today. There is another major energy running through the day that is much more positive. This aspect is very good for almost any activity one may be involved in. It is especially good for the uses of energy and power where electricity, electronic media, technology and magic are concerned. It is also great for any kind of fun, stimulating and unusual activities. Aside from the major energies, there may be scattered minor irritability from the early predawn through the early morning. Moods will improve through the mid morning, and this should run through much of the afternoon. Watch the late afternoon for a brief period of relationship issues that may return in the late night.

Saturday, 21st

High energy from yesterday will tend to linger through today. There is scattered minor irritability through the early to mid predawn. Moods will be much more positive through the early to mid morning. Be open to the intuitive process. Take a disciplined approach through the afternoon and it should be possible to get a lot done. There may be a brief period of exaggerated emotional responses in the mid afternoon, but this will probably pass unnoticed. The early evening brings back the good moods, but things will take a nosedive in the late night, and this will not be the most positive Saturday night you've ever experienced. You may want to pack it in early as there is a period of very bad moods as the Moon goes void of course at 11:29.

Sunday, 22nd

Late Saturday night social scenes will not be positively energized into today's predawn, which starts out with a period of potentially really rotten moods. Late last night's Moon void of course period ends at 1:17 this morning when the Moon enters Scorpio. At that point the energy will lift

☿	∠	♄	4:56PM
♂	#	♇	6:13
☽	△	☿	9:31
☉	→	♌	10:00
☽	⚺	♃	10:02

and general moods will tend to become more intense. There are four major energies running through today. The first easily brings problems to communication and transportation, especially where people run into restriction and frustration. The second is somewhat more seriously cautionary. Be on the lookout for secret and coercive activities up to and including violence. Do not let minor disputes escalate, and under no circumstances allow yourself to be drawn into altercations with strangers. The third is the Sun's entry into the fixed fire sign Leo, which signals the beginning of the middle portion of the summer season. During this time you will want to continue to work hard cultivating the major projects begun back at the Vernal Equinox. The fourth, which peaks in tomorrow's predawn, stimulates a great deal of activity in communication and transportation. Don't bite off more than you can chew or promise too much.

Monday, 23rd

☽	∠	♇	1:10
☿	⚻	♃	2:44
☽	#	☉	2:56
☽	#	☿	10:11
☽	//	♃	10:57
☽	△	♅	2:16PM
☽	☍	♂	6:42
☽	□	♇	7:57

High energy from yesterday will remain very much with us through today. Reread and apply. Be especially watchful for the excessive energy involving communication and transportation. People will be trying to say and do too much, and things will easily spin out of control. Aside from the major energy watch the early through mid predawn for minor coercive irritability. The late predawn through early morning is open, but the late morning may have minor scratchy attitudes. Take an innovative approach through the afternoon. Watch for a downturn through evening with aggressiveness and spaciness. Relax, take it easy.

Tuesday, 24th

☽	□	♄	3:30
☽	⚼	☿	6:54
☿	#	♃	6:55
☽	⚺	♇	7:07
☽	→	♐	1:28PM
♂	□	♇	4:09
☽	△	☉	4:51
☽	□	♀	7:02

Most of today's predawn is open, but watch the late predawn for irritability and hard attitudes. The Moon will be void of course today from 3:30 this morning until 1:28 this afternoon when it enters Sagittarius. At that point the energy will lift noticeably and general moods will tend to become more expansive and open to a wide range of ideas. There are two major energies running through today. The first continues the excessive communication and transportation energy from a couple days back. Get a lot done, but be realistic. The second is much more seriously cautionary. Be very careful around water and hot and caustic liquids and gases. Also beware of sudden spacy violence and those overdoing recreational substances. Moods will be positive following the void of course through the late afternoon, but watch for relationship issues in the evening.

July 2007   Pacific Time

Wednesday, 25th

☽ ☌ ♃ 9:24
☽ ⚻ ☿ 3:50PM
☉ ⚺ ♀ 11:14

There is a major energy coming into focus throughout the day that can be very positive for relationships. Light will be shed and greater understanding available. Make a positive gesture. Today's predawn is open. Take an expansive approach through most of the workday. Watch the mid to late afternoon for a brief period of minor erratic irritability, but this will pass quickly if it is noticed at all.

Thursday, 26th

☽ ☐ ☉ 12:28
☽ □ ♅ 1:05
☽ ✶ ♆ 6:31
☉ ☐ ♅ 8:16
☽ ⚻ ♂ 8:47
☽ △ ♄ 2:24PM
☽ ☌ ♀ 5:13
☽ — ♑ 11:20

Positive relationship energy mentioned yesterday will remain with us through today. Make good use of it. There is another major energy that easily brings about erratic and bizarre behavior of all kinds. Watch for the crazies. This energy also stimulates problems with and for authority, who can turn in an instant in any direction. Don't mess with the boss and don't get caught in anyone else's crossfire. Today's early predawn has an erratic irritability. Moods will improve through the very early morning, but watch the mid morning for erratic emotional reactions and aggressiveness. Moods will lighten through the afternoon and a disciplined approach will yield the best results. Be aware that the Moon will be void of course from 5:13 this afternoon until 11:20 tonight when it enters Capricorn. At that point the energy will lift and general moods will tend to become more down to earth and concerned with accomplishment.

Friday, 27th

☽ △ ♀ 4:53
☽ ⚻ ☉ 7:10
♀ ℞ 10:28
☽ ⚼ ♆ 10:42
☽ ☐ ♂ 2:31PM
☽ ⚺ ♃ 6:07
☽ ☐ ♄ 6:42

Venus turns retrograde today and backs up in our sky until September 8th. During the Venus retrograde what can easily occur is that people and relationships from the past reappear. When this happens, there is sometimes a tendency to rekindle old flames. This seems like a good idea until the retro ends and we remember why the relationship ended in the first place. On the other hand, this energy can be used positively to learn from past relationships. Most of today's predawn is open. Moods will improve from the late predawn to the early morning, but there may be some erratic irritability in the early morning. The late morning has minor spaciness and the mid afternoon chips in with a brief period of aggressiveness. The evening is mixed. Take an expansive approach and avoid hard attitudes.

Saturday, 28th

☽ ☍ ☿ 7:26
☽ ☐ ♀ 8:29

There are three major energies running through today. The first easily brings problems to relationships. Watch for min-

☽	⚹	♅	9:00
☽	⚺	♆	2:09PM
☿	∠	♀	4:07
☽	△	♂	7:22
☿	△	♅	8:23
☽	∠	♃	9:21
☽	⚻	♄	10:14

or disagreements tending to escalate unreasonably. With Venus retrograde, there will be a tendency to compare partners from the past to partners present. Don't say it and try not to even think it. The second is very positive for communication and transportation, especially where electricity, electronic media and technology are involved. This energy is also positive for any sort of fun, unusual and stimulating activities you may be involved in. You will notice energy levels rising throughout today as tomorrow's full Moon rolls in. Have fun tonight, but be aware that the Moon will be void of course from 7:22 tonight into tomorrow morning.

Sunday, 29th

☽	⚺	♇	12:18
☽	–	♒	6:13
☽	⚻	♀	11:19
☽	∠	♅	11:53
☽	#	☿	2:42PM
☽	//	♃	4:42
☽	☍	☉	5:47
☽	⚹	♃	11:57

Last night's Moon void of course period runs through the predawn and finally ends at 6:13 this morning when the Moon enters Aquarius. At that point the energy will lift noticeably and general moods will tend to become more independent and free-thinking. Today is full Moon day. It is exact at 5:47 this afternoon. Remember that full Moons are always high energy and deserve to be approached with respect. Relax and take it easy through the void of course. Aside from the major energy most of the morning is open, but watch the midday for relationship issues and minor erratic emotional responses. This will pass, but a similar minor energy returns in the mid afternoon. The evening into the nighttime is open. Enjoy the high energy.

Monday, 30th

☽	∠	♇	2:52
☽	#	☉	7:16
☽	#	♂	10:15
☿	⚻	♆	12:58PM
☽	⚺	♅	2:12
☽	//	♇	4:27
☽	☌	♆	7:07
☽	⚻	☿	8:00
☽	//	♆	11:45

Consider the full Moon to run through today and much of tomorrow at least. There is another major energy running through the day that brings out the space cases. Watch for those overindulging recreational substances and the otherwise out of it. Be especially careful in traffic. Today's predawn starts out with good moods, but watch the mid predawn for a brief minor coercive irritability. Make good choices through most of the morning and watch the late morning for aggressive attitudes. Moods will improve through the afternoon. Take an innovative and communicative approach. Be open to the intuitive process through the evening and watch the late night for minor erratic irritability, which will pass quickly if it is noticed at all.

Tuesday, 31st

☽	#	♄	2:31
☽	□	♂	2:54
☽	☍	♄	3:27

There are two major energies running throughout today. The first is significantly cautionary. Watch for people running into restrictions and frustrations, and having difficulty

July 2007 — Pacific Time

☽	⚹	♆	4:55
☽	−	♓	10:39
☽	☍	♀	3:09PM
♂	□	♄	4:59
☉	∥	♂	10:25

not acting out on them. Minor disputes can easily escalate out of control and consequences will be harsher and longer lasting than usual. The second is positive for making beginnings in projects involving energy and power. These energies are related, but the differences are clear and the right choices will be needed. Watch the mid predawn for hard attitudes and aggressiveness. Moods will improve in the late predawn, but be aware that the Moon will be void of course this morning from 4:55 until 10:39 when it enters Pisces. At that point the energy will lift noticeably and general moods will tend to become more mellow, if a bit spacy. The early afternoon is open, but watch the mid afternoon for relationship issues. The evening opens up again.

August 2007

Overview

As August opens, the Saturn opposed Neptune will have given way to the trine to Pluto. It peaks early in the month, but remains throughout and this is the energy that signals the end of the current round of international conflict, and with any luck, a peace of sorts in the U.S. culture war. This will not all occur overnight, but will be a couple years in the working out. There will, nonetheless, be certain indications that can be taken seriously. Of course, there are still people fighting the battle from the last time we had these energies back in the '60s and '70s. Just so, there will be holdouts from this go around, and we'll be decades seeing the very end, if indeed we ever do. For the majority, however, this is the beginning of the end. Now is not the time for complacency. Most of those committed to prolonging things will not quit easily, and don't really care much what the planets have to say. Things will heat up next month and it remains vitally important to continue participating in whatever prayer and meditation for peace events get organized.

August will be a high energy month on the personal level. There are very few days that do not have major energies to deal with and there are many days with multiple majors that sometimes are quite contradictory. The first week has a string of high energy days and there is little let up the second. You will want to remember that Venus will be retrograde all month. Relationships will be spotlighted and the temptation to restart or dwell on old unions will be great. Remember to keep comparisons to yourself and be especially careful around the 7th. Be more attentive than usual with what you start around the new Moon which is exact on the 12th. There are many more days that you will want to read ahead and plan for dealing with. The most significant daytime Moon void of course periods are on the 10th–11th, and the 24th–25th.

Wednesday, 1st

☽	⚼	☿	1:32
☽	⚻	☉	1:38
☽	□	♃	3:45
☽	#	♀	10:05
☽	//	♅	11:36
☽	☌	♅	5:34PM
☿	⚼	♃	6:34
♂	⚻	♇	8:00

There are three major energies running through today. The first continues the positive energy mentioned yesterday. Make new beginnings of all kinds. The second can bring problems to communication and transportation, especially where people attempt to say and do too much. Get a lot done, but be realistic. The second is much more cautionary. Watch for secret and coercive activities up to and including violence. This can pop up suddenly and from unexpected

☽ ⚺ ♆ 10:23

directions. Do not let minor disputes escalate, and under no circumstances allow yourself to be drawn into altercations with strangers. There is scattered minor irritability from the early through mid predawn. Most of the morning opens up, but watch the late morning for minor relationship issues. Take an innovative approach through the afternoon and evening.

Thursday, 2nd

☽	⚼	☉	4:58
☽	△	☿	6:48
☽	⚻	♄	7:05
☽	□	♇	8:00
☿	#	♃	8:08
☉	△	♃	8:12
☽	⚹	♂	8:36
☿	⚺	♄	9:07
☽	–	♈	1:42PM
☿	⚻	♇	3:53
☽	⚻	♀	5:23
☽	∠	♆	11:41

There are five major energies running throughout the day. The first is a continuation of the energy from the past several days for an excess of activity involving communication and transportation. Again, don't make promises you can't deliver on. The second is high positive energy, pure and simple. This aspect is excellent for anything one may be involved in. The third is very positive for communication and transportation, especially where deliberate, disciplined steps are being taken. This energy is very good for negotiation and coming to long term agreement. The fourth, however, is somewhat contradictory, and easily leads to the unexpected exposure of things normally kept secret and hidden. Guard your secrets and observe as others' are revealed. The fifth once again adds positive energy for communication and transportation. This will obviously be a day for good choices. Be aware of and be sure to work around the Moon void of course period running from 8:36 this morning until 1:42 this afternoon when the Moon enters Aries. At that point the energy will lift noticeably and general moods will tend to become more assertive and aggressive.

Friday, 3rd

☽	#	♅	2:34
☿	⚹	♂	2:51
☽	//	♀	3:13
☽	△	♃	6:29
☽	△	☉	8:07
☽	⚼	♄	8:37
☽	∠	♂	11:08
☽	⚼	♀	6:11PM
☽	⚺	♅	8:07

High energy from yesterday will remain very much with us through today. Make good use of the positive, but be sure to factor in the cautionary. There is another major energy coming into focus today that continues yesterday's cautions. Continue to keep the eyes and ears open as light is shed on things normally kept beneath the surface. This version of the energy also easily leads to problems with and for authority. Watch for attempts at regime change and don't get caught up in other people's machinations. At the same time, use this energy to look within and come to deeper self understanding. Aside from the major energies, there may be erratic emotional responses in the mid predawn. Moods will improve markedly through the early to mid morning for all but those giving way to hard attitudes. There may be minor aggressiveness at the midday, but this will pass quickly.

Pacific Time   August 2007

☽	✶	♆	12:55
☉	⚻	♇	1:11
☽	⚻	♃	7:44
☽	△	♄	10:06
☿	—	♌	10:14
☽	∥	♄	10:27
☽	△	♇	10:31
☽	⚼	♂	1:37PM
☽	⚺	♆	1:58
☽	—	♉	4:15
♀	⚺	♅	4:59
☽	□	☿	5:13
☽	△	♀	6:55
☽	⚺	♇	9:09
☽	⚼	♅	9:20
☽	∥	☉	11:30

The very early evening may have a brief period of relationship issues, but good moods should dominate the late night. Have fun.

Saturday, 4th
Continue to observe the cautionary energy from yesterday involving the exposure of secrets and potential problems with authority. There are three more major energies. The first indicates a general shift in communication and transportation toward a more intense and personal mode. The second easily brings problems to relationships. Watch for sudden irrational and unrealistic demands for change. If problems pop up in this area, switch immediately to damage control. On higher octaves, this energy can be fun and stimulating, but needs to be handled carefully. The third, which peaks early tomorrow, is positive for communication in relationships. Remember, however, that Venus is retrograde. You may well hear from or be thinking about people from the past. Be willing to learn from this, but careful about reengaging. Be aware that the Moon will be void of course from 10:31 this morning until 4:15 this afternoon when it enters Taurus. At that point the energy will lift noticeably and general moods will tend to become more down to earth and concerned with enjoyment. Good moods should run through the midday and much of the afternoon. The evening through the late night is mixed. Have fun, but good choices will be needed.

☿	⚼	♀	4:00
☽	∥	♂	7:16
☽	✶	♃	9:01
☽	⚻	♇	11:47
☽	□	☉	2:19PM
☽	∥	☿	3:53
☽	⚺	♃	8:07
☿	⚻	♅	10:26
☽	✶	♅	10:37

Sunday, 5th
High energy from yesterday will tend to remain with us through today. Make the right choices in dealing with it. There is another major energy running through the day that can bring problems to communication and transportation, especially where electricity and electronic media are involved. Be careful in traffic. This aspect also brings out the crazies, so if you see someone whose cheese seems to have slipped off their cracker, that is probably the case. Aside from the major energies, today's predawn is open. Take an active approach through the early morning, but watch the mid morning to midday for exaggerated emotional responses and a coercive irritability. The mid afternoon features a period of very bad moods. Things should lighten up through the evening into the late night.

Monday, 6th

| ☽ | □ | ♆ | 3:27 |

The cautionary energy mentioned yesterday will linger

Astro-Weather

August 2007   Pacific Time

♄	△	♆	3:35
☽	⚻	♆	1:10PM
☽	□	♄	1:15
☽	☌	♂	6:49
☽	–	♊	7:01
♃	D		7:05
☽	□	♀	8:25
☉	#	♆	10:35
♂	–	♊	11:01

through the day. Reread and apply. There are three more major energies to deal with today. The first is a long range outer planet aspect that relates to the eventual end to the current round of international conflict that came to public attention on 9/11 of 2001. There should be some movement in the right direction reflected in the media in the weeks surrounding this date. It will be two or three more years before all of this plays out. The second is a reprise of the energy for the exposure of secrets and problems with authority from a few days back. Read back and extend the cautions. The third, which occurs in tomorrow's early pre-dawn, indicates a general shift in the way energy and power are used toward a more communicative mode. Minor aspects are of very little help through the day and good choices will be needed. Be aware of a short Moon void of course period this evening from 6:49 until 7:01 when the Moon enters Gemini. At that point the energy will lift and general moods will tend to become more communicative. Watch the later evening for potential relationship issues.

Tuesday, 7th

☽	✶	☿	4:23
☽	☍	♃	11:58
♀	□	♂	4:36PM
☽	✶	☉	9:07

High cautionary energy from yesterday will remain with us through today. Continue to be careful with it. There is another major energy running through today that definitely bears watching. This aspect easily stimulates conflict in relationships. Remember that Venus is retrograde. This combination will bring about sitcom level issues. The mere passing faintest glimmer of a reference to a past relationship can turn into Armageddon in an instant. Remember that you are not a cast member of Seinfeld. Worlds colliding are not nearly as funny when it happens in your life. Aside from the major energy, moods should be more positive than otherwise, possibly leading one to think that such a reference might be well received. It won't. Choices.

Wednesday, 8th

☽	□	♅	1:41
☽	△	♆	6:37
☽	∠	☿	10:33
☽	☍	♇	4:33PM
☽	✶	♄	5:11
♀	–	♌	6:09
☽	✶	♀	10:27
☽	–	♋	10:36
☿	∥	♂	10:45

Watch for fallout from yesterday's problem relationship energy through today and perhaps tomorrow as well. Be kind to those caught up in it. There is another major energy that indicates a general shift in relationship energy toward a more intense and personal mode. This is Venus retrograding back into Leo. Expect relationship issues to be taken more personally than usual. Aside from the major energy, watch the mid to late predawn for minor erratic irritability. Take an intuitive approach to the morning. Watch for minor irritability at the midday, but most of the rest of the after-

☽ ⚼ ♂	12:57	
☽ ∠ ☉	1:00	
☿ △ ♃	8:36	
☽ □ ♆	8:38	
☽ ⚻ ♃	3:59PM	
☽ ⚼ ☿	5:17	
☽ ∠ ♄	7:39	
☽ ∠ ♀	11:51	

☿ □ ♆	2:49	
☽ ∠ ♂	4:37	
☽ ⚼ ☉	5:21	
☽ △ ♅	5:57	
☽ ⚻ ♆	11:04	
☉ ⚻ ♅	1:27PM	
☽ □ ♃	6:37	
☽ ⚻ ♀	9:23	
☽ ⚼ ♄	10:36	

☽ ⚼ ♀	1:37	
☽ – ♌	3:42	
☽ □ ♅	8:46	
☽ ⚹ ♂	8:51	

noon is open. The late afternoon to early evening is mixed; take a disciplined and friendly approach. Be aware of a very short Moon void of course period late tonight, running from 10:27 until 10:36 when the Moon enters Cancer, and general moods will tend to become more sensitive and protective.

Thursday, 9th

There are two major energies running through today. The first is excellent for any activity involving transportation and communication. This is a go-for-it day and much may be accomplished. The second is more cautionary and easily leads to the exposure of things normally kept beneath the surface. This energy can also bring about sarcasm and general nastiness. These two energies provide two very clear choices. Be careful in traffic. Aside from the major energies the early predawn is mixed. Take an active, communicative approach and watch for minor irritability. The early to mid morning may have a brief period of spaciness, but this will pass quickly if it's noticed at all. The late morning through much of the afternoon is open. The late afternoon is more positive. Take a communicative approach but watch evening for minor hard attitudes. There may also be relationship issues in the very late night.

Friday, 10th

The cautionary energy mentioned yesterday will remain with us today. Reread and apply. Once again, be careful in traffic and offer no single digit salutes. There is another major energy running through the day that brings out the crazies. Watch for erratic and bizarre behavior of all kinds. If someone appears to be off their rocker, trust your instinct. This energy also brings problems with and for authority. Things can change in an instant. Don't mess with the boss and stay out of other people's crossfire. Moods will be predominantly positive through most of the predawn. Be aware that the Moon will be void of course from 5:57 this morning through much of tomorrow's predawn. Try to keep your head down, relax, and tend to old business through the workday. This may not be the most positive social Friday night in history.

Saturday, 11th

Yesterday's long Moon void of course period runs through much of today's predawn and finally ends at 3:42 this morning when the Moon enters Leo. At that point the energy will lift noticeably for those up and around and general

☽	#	♃	2:08PM
☽	△	♃	9:49
☽	//	♂	11:09

moods will tend to become more intense and concerned with self. Yesterday's cautionary energy will remain with us through today and should be taken into account. You will notice energy levels rising throughout the day as tomorrow's new Moon rolls in. The mid morning has a brief period of mixed energy. Take a fun and active approach and sidestep any minor erratic irritability. Good moods should run through the rest of the day and into the late night. Have fun, but be careful and remember the new Moon.

Sunday, 12th

☽	⚼	♇	12:35
☽	☌	☿	9:13
☽	//	☿	10:10
☽	⚻	♅	12:11PM
☽	#	♇	3:00
☉	#	♆	3:06
☽	☌	☉	4:02
☽	☍	♆	5:31
☽	#	♆	10:39
☽	//	☉	11:07

Today is new Moon day. It is exact at 4:02 this afternoon. Remember that what you start at new Moon brings results at the next full Moon. This particular new to full period bears watching. Try to take a disciplined approach and avoid erratic behavior, spaciness, and overindulgence of recreational substances. The coming full Moon is an eclipse which will serve to intensify the results of what you start now. There are two other major energies to deal with today. The first does easily lead to spaciness and intoxication. Manage yourself and keep an eye out for the space cases who will be present in full force. The second easily brings problems to communication and transportation, especially where electricity, electronic media, and technology are involved. This energy also stimulates erratic behavior in general. This will be a day for real good choices.

Monday, 13th

☿	⚻	♅	3:37
☽	△	♇	4:23
☽	//	♄	4:36
☽	☌	♄	6:15
☽	☌	♀	6:34
☽	→	♍	11:03
☉	☍	♆	11:25
♀	☌	♄	12:15PM
☽	□	♂	7:24

Consider the new Moon to remain with us through today and well into tomorrow. Be good. The cautionary energy mentioned yesterday will remain with us today. Reread and apply the warnings. Be especially careful in traffic. There are three more major energies running through the day, all of them of the cautionary persuasion. The first brings out the space cases in a major way. Anyone who seems seriously out of it quite likely is. This energy also brings about problems with and for authority. Watch for leadership to have a shaky grip on reality. The second would normally be positive for making new beginnings in and strengthening and solidifying relationships. It may still work for that, but remember that Venus is retrograde. This is an energy with which people will be tempted to take the leap and reestablish old relationships. What often occurs is that when Venus turns direct they remember why their relationship ended in the first place. The third easily leads to the exposure of things normally kept secret and hidden. Observe.

Pacific Time   August 2007

This energy also easily leads to problems with communication and transportation, especially where people become coercive, pushy, and engaged in nasty attitudes. Do be aware that the Moon will be void of course this morning from 6:34 until 11:03 when it enters Virgo. At that point the energy will lift and general moods will tend to be more discerning and concerned with detail.

Tuesday, 14th

☿	#	♆	2:32
☽	□	♃	6:07
☿	☍	♆	1:09PM
☽	#	♅	2:11
☽	//	♀	3:02
☽	☍	♅	8:57

The high cautionary energy from yesterday will remain very much with us through today. Reread and apply the warnings carefully. There is another major energy running through the day that adds even more spaciness. Be very careful in any activity involving communication and transportation. Watch for the inebriated and otherwise out of it. Be very careful in traffic. Minor aspects are of no help and this will be another day where choices are very important.

Wednesday, 15th

☽	⊼	♆	2:35
☽	⊻	☿	5:16
☽	⊻	☉	6:00
♀	△	♇	6:43
☉	☌	☿	12:56PM
☽	⊻	♀	1:42
☽	□	♆	2:02
☽	⊻	♄	4:39
☽	--	♎	9:04

Watch for the high cautionary energy from the past few days to linger through today. There are two more major energies. The first can be very positive for taking relationships to deeper levels. There is a stronger sexual component than usual with this energy, however, and it should be handled carefully. Also remember that Venus is retrograde and falling into something may be easy to do, but climbing out might be much more difficult. The second is positive for looking within and coming to greater self-understanding. The early predawn is open. Good moods should run from the early morning through the early afternoon. Get anything important done before 2:02 this afternoon as the Moon will be void of course from then until 9:04 tonight when it enters Libra. At that point energy will lift noticeably and general moods will tend to become more concerned with balance and beauty.

Thursday, 16th

☽	⚼	♆	8:05
☽	△	♂	9:01
☽	#	♀	12:31PM
☽	//	♅	12:49
☽	∠	☉	2:12
☿	#	♆	3:16
☽	∠	☿	4:51
☽	✶	♃	5:06
☽	∠	♀	6:01

There are three major energies to deal with today. The first continues the spacy energy from the past several days. Watch for the out of it by any means and be especially careful in traffic. The second stimulates communication in relationships. New beginnings would normally be indicated, but once again remember that Venus is retrograde. Learn from the past; don't try to return to it. The third easily brings about erratic behavior in relationships. Just when you think things are going one way, you find them going the

☿	☌	♀	10:27
☽	∠	♄	10:48

other. Watch for sudden unrealistic and unreasonable demands for change. Damage control. Minor aspects are mixed throughout the day. With the right choices, good moods will be available. With the wrong ones ...

Friday, 17th

♀	#	♅	7:35
☽	⚻	♅	8:11
☿	△	♇	10:23
☉	//	♄	10:58
☽	△	♆	2:04PM
☽	⚼	♂	4:45
☉	☌	♀	8:40
☽	#	☉	10:39
☽	⚹	♀	10:41
☽	⚹	☉	10:59
☽	#	♄	11:17
☽	∠	♃	11:21

The high energy continues to roll through today. Remain watchful for recent cautionary energies and know that there are three more major energies that will be active. The first is excellent for communication on deep levels. Information usually kept secret and hidden will be much more accessible. The second is very good for initiating projects involving self-discipline, authority, older people, and traditional matters. Build a firm foundation. The third sheds light on relationships and aesthetic concerns. Yet again, remember that Venus is retrograde. Learn from the past, but it is probably best to leave it there. Aside from the major energies, minor aspects are mixed at best and good choices will be needed througn the daytime. Moods will improve and become much more positive in the late night. Have fun, but be careful.

Saturday, 18th

☽	#	☿	1:57
☽	⚹	♇	1:57
☽	⚹	☿	5:05
☽	⚹	♄	5:21
☿	☌	♄	6:44
☽	//	♆	6:50
☽	—	♏	9:13
☽	⚼	♅	2:23PM
☽	//	♇	3:07
☿	//	♄	10:24

High energy from yesterday will remain with us through today. Maximize the positive and minimize the cautionary. There are two other major energies running through today that actually combine into one. This energy is much like yesterday's for initiating projects involving self-discipline, authority, older people, and traditional matters. This energy is more communicative, however, and may involve negotiation and coming to long term agreement. Good moods should dominate the predawn. There is some potential minor irritability, but this should pass unnoticed and good moods will extend into the early morning. The Moon will be void of course this morning, however, from 5:21 until 9:13 when it enters Scorpio. At this point the energy will lift noticeably and general moods will become more intense. Relax and take it easy through the void of course. Much of the afternoon is open, but the mid afternoon may have a brief period of erratic emotional responses. Make good choices to get the most out of this day. Have fun tonight, but be careful.

Sunday, 19th

☽	⚻	♂	12:46
☽	⚺	♃	5:48

High energy mentioned over the past two days will remain with us through today. Make good use of it. There are three

Pacific Time   August 2007

☿	—	♍	6:00
☽	∠	♆	8:17
☉	△	♆	11:14
☽	#	♂	1:56PM
☽	∥	♃	6:46
☽	△	♅	8:38
☉	∥	☿	11:27

more major energies to deal with as well. The first indicates a general shift in communication and transportation activities toward a more discerning and concerned with detail mode. The second sheds light on things normally kept secret and hidden, but in a more positive way than usual. Stay awake as there will be much to learn and needed changes may be better understood and implemented. The third is positive for looking within and coming to greater self understanding. Those involved in transformational practices should make the most of this day. Make the right choices.

Monday, 20th

☽	□	♆	2:34
☽	□	♀	8:19
☽	⚻	♆	2:29PM
☽	□	☉	4:54
☽	□	♄	6:33
☽	—	♐	9:43

High positive energy from yesterday will remain with us today and tomorrow at least. Continue to make good use of it, but know that there are irritable minor aspects running through the day as well. Watch the mid predawn for a period of spaciness. The early to mid morning may have relationship issues. The late morning to mid afternoon is open, but watch the late afternoon through early evening for a period of potentially very bad moods and hard attitudes. Also be aware that the Moon will be void of course tonight from 6:33 until 9:43 when it enters Sagittarius. At that point the energy will lift noticeably and general moods will become more expansive and open to wide range of ideas.

Tuesday, 21st

☽	□	☿	5:19
☽	☍	♂	4:13PM
☉	☌	♄	4:28
☽	☌	♃	6:06

The high positive energy for dealing with self-discipline, authority, older people and traditional matters returns very strongly through today. If you have all your ducks in a row, you may think about approaching the boss. Most of the predawn is open, but watch the late predawn for a brief period of irritability. Go for it through the workday, but watch the late afternoon for some potential for some minor aggressiveness. Take an expansive approach to the early evening

Wednesday, 22nd

☽	□	♅	8:06
☽	✶	♆	1:51PM
☽	△	♀	4:48

Today's predawn is open. Watch the early to mid morning for a brief period of erratic emotional reactions. Take an intuitive approach through the early afternoon. Good moods should run through the late afternoon and early evening. The late night is open again. Choose well and have a good time today.

Thursday, 23rd

| ☽ | ☌ | ♆ | 1:22 |

There are two major energies running through today. The

Astro-Weather   101

☉	→	♍	5:07
☽	△	♄	5:54
☽	→	♑	8:18
☽	△	☉	8:34
♂	☍	♃	9:03
☽	∠	♆	6:26PM
☽	⚼	♀	8:08

first is the Sun's entry into the mutable earth sign Virgo as the final third of the summer season begins. During this time you will want to pay particular attention to the details of the projects begun back at the Vernal Equinox back in March. The second is high energy pure and simple. The problem is that there is too much energy and people can easily get carried away. Take an active approach, but keep a grip. Be aware that the Moon will be void of course this morning from 5:54 until 8:18 when it enters Capricorn. At that point the energy will lift noticeably and general moods will tend to become more assertive and aggressive. Fortunately, a period of good moods follows right behind the end of the void of course and should make everything more manageable. Carefully get a lot done the rest of the workday and watch the evening for spaciness and relationship issues.

Friday, 24th

☽	△	☿	1:33
☽	⚺	♃	3:51
☽	⚻	♂	4:43
☽	⚼	♄	10:18
☽	⚼	☉	2:52PM
☽	⚹	♅	4:40
☿	□	♃	6:03
☽	⚺	♆	10:07
☽	⚻	♀	10:43

There are two major energies running through today and tomorrow. They combine, along with the high energy from yesterday, to add up to problems with communication and transportation. Watch for people to attempt to say and do too much with resulting frustration. Those acting out on this can be pushed all too easily all the way to violence. This can be a very positive complex with which much may be accomplished, but it needs to be handled very carefully. Minor aspects are mixed. With the right choices, this can be a day to remember. With the wrong choices, it can easily be a day you'll want to forget. Be especially careful out in the world tonight and be very vigilant in traffic. Also be aware that the Moon will be void of course from 4:40 this afternoon through much of the daytime tomorrow.

Saturday, 25th

☽	∠	♃	7:25
☿	□	♂	8:59
☽	⚺	♇	9:01
☽	⚼	♂	9:25
☽	⚼	☿	9:28
☽	⚻	♄	1:49PM
♀	☍	♆	2:49
☽	→	♒	3:34
☽	∠	♅	7:38
☽	⚻	☉	8:03

Yesterday's Moon void of course will run through much of the daytime and finally end at 3:34 this afternoon when the Moon enters Aquarius. At that point the energy will lift very noticeably and general moods will tend to become more independent and free thinking. Late Friday night social situations will be strongly energized through today's predawn. Late nighters will want to deal carefully with others and not let minor disputes escalate. The high energy, that can be either very positive or very not, will remain very much with us through today. It is joined by another major energy that easily brings problems to relationships. Watch for spaciness and confusion, especially where people and issues from the past are involved. The Moon being void of course through

Pacific Time   August 2007

☽	∥	♃	1:09
☽	#	♂	2:09
☽	✶	♃	10:07
☽	∠	♇	11:33
☽	△	♂	1:09PM
☽	⊼	☿	4:00
☽	⋆	♅	9:47

Sunday, 26th

so much of the day may serve to put at least a bit of a damper on trouble. This will be a very high energy social Saturday night, but one to be exceedingly careful with.

Watch for the energy from the past several days to remain very much with us through today. You will also notice energy levels rising throughout the day as the coming full Moon eclipse rolls in. There is another major energy today that peaks in tomorrow's late predawn which would normally be very good for communication in and making new starts in relationships. Remember that Venus remains retrograde for another couple of weeks and think seriously before starting up again with someone from the past. Aside from the major energies, minor aspects are mixed. Good moods will be available, but the right choices need to be made.

Monday, 27th

☽	∥	♇	1:02
☽	☍	♀	1:49
☿	∥	♀	2:56
☽	☌	♆	2:59
☽	∥	♆	7:52
☽	✶	♇	1:20PM
☽	#	♄	4:15
☽	☍	♄	6:23
☽	—	♓	7:33

The full Moon is exact in tomorrow's mid predawn making tonight and tomorrow the most intense of the full Moon period. Remember that full Moons are always high energy and deserve to be approached with respect. This particular full Moon is an eclipse. That, along with some of the surrounding energies, makes it more intense than usual. General energy levels will be very high and people will tend to be more volatile, so do try to keep a grip on yourself and be careful in your dealings with others. There is a short Moon void of course period tonight, running from 6:23 until 7:33 when the Moon enters Pisces. At that point general moods will tend to become a little more spacy, but the intensity of the full Moon will remain.

Tuesday, 28th

☽	☍	☉	3:34
☽	☍	☉	3:37
☽	#	☉	4:20
♂	#	♃	7:13
☿	☍	♅	12:39PM
☽	#	♀	12:51
☽	□	♃	1:25
☽	□	♂	6:18
☽	#	☿	6:20
☽	∥	♅	6:36
☿	#	♅	8:41

The full Moon is exact at 3:34 this morning and this will be a very intense day for most people. There are three more major energies to deal with. The first is a reprise of some of the very high energy from a few days ago. This, coupled with the full Moon, will have some people barely able to contain themselves. Do not tease or otherwise provoke those seeming close to the edge, as they may well jump off and pull you down along with them. Play the peacemaker and you may be able to do a lot of good. The second and third combine into one that will stimulate a great deal of activity in communication and transportation, especially where electricity, electronic media and technology are in-

Astro-Weather   103

August 2007 — Pacific Time

volved. Problems can set in where people become so intent on making their point or getting something done that they become willing to run over any thing or any person that they perceive as in their way. On higher octaves, this is very powerful energy for those involved in magical practices. Minor aspects are of no help today and good choices are imperative.

Wednesday, 29th

☽ ☌ ♅   12:14
☽ ☍ ☿   1:52
☽ ⚻ ♀   2:46
☽ ⚺ ♆   5:17
☿ ⚺ ♀   8:12
☽ □ ♇   3:21PM
☽ ⚻ ♄   8:41
☽ – ♈   9:24

Consider the full Moon and attendant high energy to remain with us through today and well into tomorrow. There is another major energy today that is positive for communication in relationships. Remember that Venus is retrograde and be very careful of reengaging in old relationships. With this energy, it may be possible find closure or to finally let go of things from past relationships, and that would be good use of it. There may be some minor irritability in the early to mid predawn. Be open to the intuitive process in the late predawn. Most of the workday period is open, but there may be a brief period of irritability in the mid afternoon. Be aware that the Moon will be void of course from 3:21 this afternoon until 9:24 tonight when it enters Aries. At that point the energy will lift and general moods will tend to become more assertive and aggressive.

Thursday. 30th

☽ □ ♀   2:50
☽ ∠ ♆   5:54
☿ ⚻ ♆   6:14
☽ ∥ ☿   7:10
☽ ⚻ ☉   8:43
☽ # ♅   11:08
☽ △ ♃   3:05PM
☽ ∥ ♀   6:06
☽ □ ♄   9:29
☽ ∥ ☉   9:36
☽ ✶ ♂   9:43

There is a major energy running through today that easily brings problems to communication and transportation especially where the inebriated and otherwise out of it are involved. Watch for misunderstanding and confusion in the transfer of information and be especially careful in traffic. Aside from the major energy, the early predawn is open. Watch the mid through late predawn for minor relationship issues and spaciness. Try to take a communicative approach through the morning, but remember the major energy and be very clear in your meaning. There may be minor irritability in the mid morning and erratic emotional responses in the late afternoon to midday. Most of the rest of the afternoon is open and good moods should run through the mid afternoon. The late night is mixed. Take a fun and active approach and avoid a tendency toward hard attitudes.

Friday, 31st

☽ ⚺ ♅   1:24
☽ △ ♀   2:50
☽ ✶ ♆   6:26

Today we get a break from major energies. Good moods will run through the predawn and very early morning. Take a fun and friendly approach and be open to the intuitive pro-

Pacific Time   August 2007

☽	⚻	☿	9:39
☽	☐	☉	11:01
☽	//	♄	12:17PM
☽	☐	♃	3:47
☽	△	♇	4:31
☽	#	♆	9:09
☽	△	♄	10:18
☽	—	♉	10:35
☽	∠	♂	11:21

cess. Follow guidance. There may be a downturn in the mid through late morning with erratic emotional reactions and general irritability. Take a disciplined approach through most of the afternoon. The late afternoon into the early evening lightens up and the rest of the evening is open. There may be a brief period of spaciness in the later, but this will not amount to much. Make good choices and enjoy the day. There is a very short Moon void of course period tonight from 10:18 until 10:35 when the Moon enters Taurus. At that point the energy will lift and general moods will tend to become more down to earth and concerned with enjoyment.

Astro-Weather

September 2007

Overview

As September begins, the Saturn trine Pluto from last month is still in orb but separating out. There should have been noticeable indications of the beginning of the end of the current international conflict. Nurture whatever buds of peace that have begun to open. Saturn will move on out of orb over the next couple of months, but will retro back for a final trine through the spring of next year, and that will be when the writing on the wall will be undeniable for all but the most recalcitrant die-hards among the combative elements. By late this month, Jupiter will move back into its final square to Saturn for this cycle. This will once again heat up the rhetoric and get people's knickers back into a knot. Watch as the tension rises, but know that we are now finally on the down side of all of this. Unfortunate things will still be occurring, but subconsciously at least, it is known that the end is coming. Please continue to support whatever prayer and meditation for peace efforts as get organized.

This will be a busy month on more personal levels. There is high cautionary energy over Labor Day weekend. Be very careful all the way through the 4th. Venus turns direct on the 8th. At this point people will be starting to find out if the relationship moves they've made since the retro started back on July 27th were a good idea or not. This is especially true where they have returned to old relationships. See the retrograde pages at the beginning of the book for more on these periods. There is another highly cautionary period from the 17th through 21st, at least. This is a T-square involving the Sun, Mars and Pluto. This may well produce headlines at the local as well as international levels. There are many other major energies to read ahead and be prepared for. The most significant daytime Moon void of course periods are on the 14th and the 19th. There are a few half day voids to watch for as well.

Saturday, 1st

☽	∠	♅	1:57
☽	#	♇	3:38
☽	△	☉	1:28PM
☽	⚼	☿	1:33
☉	//	♀	3:30
☽	⚻	♃	4:38
☽	⚼	♇	5:15

There is a major energy running through the day that sheds light on relationships and would normally be positive for new beginnings in them. Remember, however, that Venus remains retrograde for another few days. This energy can still be used in a positive way, but you may want to think two or three times before reinitiating old relationships. If this really is the right thing to do, this is the time for it. But is it? Learn from the past. Minor aspects are mixed. Good

Pacific Time   September 2007

moods should run through most of the daytime, especially through the afternoon. Make good choices and don't fall prey to minor irritants. Have fun tonight.

Sunday, 2nd

☽	⚺	♂	1:11
☽	⚹	♅	2:43
☽	#	♃	2:49
☽	□	♀	3:19
☽	//	♂	4:33
♄	–	♍	6:48
☽	□	♆	7:53
☽	△	☿	5:47PM
☽	⚻	♇	6:16
☿	□	♇	10:04

Late Saturday night social scenes should be positively energized well into today's predawn. Watch the late predawn through much of the morning, however, for relationship issues and spaciness. There are two major energies running through the day. The first indicates a general shift in the way foundational, structural, and discipline matters are approached toward a more discerning and detailed mode. The second easily brings problems to communication and transportation, especially where people become coercive and nasty attitudes are indulged. This energy also easily leads to the exposure of things normally kept secret and hidden. Guard your secrets and observe. Aside from the major energies, most of the daytime is open. Good moods should run in the late afternoon, but be aware that the Moon will be void of course from 5:47 this afternoon into tomorrow's predawn.

Monday, 3rd – Labor Day

☽	–	♊	12:30
☽	□	♄	12:39
♂	□	♅	1:09PM
♀	⚹	♂	4:36
☉	□	♃	5:04
☽	☍	♃	7:23
☽	□	☉	7:32

Last night's Moon void of course period ends at 12:30 this morning when the Moon enters Gemini. At that point the energy will lift and general moods will tend to become more communicative. Watch for a period of hard attitudes immediately following the void of course. There are three major energies running through the day. The first is highly cautionary. Watch for sudden, unexpected violence, freak accidents, and electrical fires. This is very explosive energy that should not be fooled around with. Do not let any minor disputes escalate. The second can be very positive for relationships. This is the energy to focus on. The third will have many people feeling positive, confident, and generally good about themselves, but easily leads to excess of all kinds. This will be a very high energy day that needs to be handled carefully. Watch the evening for exaggerated emotional responses and some very bad moods. Choices.

Tuesday, 4th

☽	□	♅	5:21
☽	⚹	♀	5:23
☽	☌	♂	6:06
♀	⚻	♅	8:23
☽	△	♆	10:47

High energy from yesterday will tend to remain very much with us through today. Reread and apply. There is another major energy that also definitely bears watching, as it easily brings problems to relationships. Watch for sudden, unrealistic and unreasonable demands for change. Erratic behavior

September 2007　　　　　　　　　　　　　　　　Pacific Time

| ☽ ☍ ♆ | 9:39PM |

should be expected, but not rewarded. Damage control. Aside from the major energies, today's predawn is open. The morning is mixed. Watch the late predawn to early morning for erratic emotional responses and choose a friendly, active approach instead. Be open to the intuitive process through the late morning. The afternoon through the early evening is open, but watch later for a brief period of coercive irritability.

Wednesday, 5th

☽ □ ☿	4:00
☽ — ♋	4:08
☽ ✶ ♄	4:46
☿ — ♎	5:02
☽ ⚼ ♀	7:16
☿ ⚻ ♄	11:05
☽ ⚻ ♆	1:00PM

High energy from the past few days is likely to linger through today. It is joined by two more major energies. The first indicates a general shift in thinking and communication toward a more balanced mode. The second can be very good for matters involving communication and transportation. Take a disciplined approach and much may be accomplished. This energy is great for negotiation and coming to long term agreement. Most of today's predawn is open but watch the late predawn for a brief period of argumentativeness. There will be a very short Moon void of course period this morning from 4:00 until 4:08 when the Moon enters Cancer. At that point the energy will lift and general moods will tend to become more sensitive and protective. Take a disciplined approach following the void of course, but watch for minor relationship issues in the early morning. There may be some minor spaciness in the early afternoon but aside from that, the rest of the daytime through the evening is open.

Thursday, 6th

☽ ⚻ ♃	12:09
☽ ✶ ☉	4:03
☿ ⚼ ♀	6:34
☽ ⚼ ♄	7:41
☽ ⚻ ♀	9:46
☽ △ ♅	10:04
☽ ⚻ ♂	1:21PM
☽ ⚻ ♆	3:46

Positive energy from yesterday will tend to linger through today. Make good use of it. There is another major energy that is more cautionary. Watch for relationship issues. We are in the last few days of the Venus Retrograde and people from the past are likely to be present in mind if not in person. Comparisons are not recommended. Try not to think it and whatever you do, don't say it. Aside from the major energies, watch the early predawn for exaggerated emotional responses. Good moods should run through the late predawn but the rest of the morning is mixed. Take a friendly, communicative and innovative approach avoiding hard attitudes. Get anything important done before 10:04 this morning as the Moon will be void of course from then through much of tomorrow morning.

Friday, 7th

☽	⚻	♇	3:13
☽	⚼	♃	3:24
♇	D		7:55
☽	∠	☉	9:24
☽	→	♌	10:00
☽	⚺	♄	11:11
☽	⚼	♅	1:16PM
☉	#	♅	1:57
☽	//	♂	3:13
☽	⚹	☿	5:11
☽	∠	♂	5:56
☽	#	♃	7:02

Yesterday's long Moon void of course runs through much of this morning and finally ends at 10:00 when the Moon enters Leo. At that point the energy will lift very noticeably and general moods will tend to become more intense and concerned with self. Relax and take it easy through the void of course but be prepared to hit the ground running as it ends. There is a major energy running through the day that is cautionary, but can be used positively. On the downside, watch for the crazies. Erratic and bizarre behavior will be noticeable. This energy also brings problems with and for authority, which can change direction without a moment's notice. On the upside, this energy can be good for the use of technology and magic. It can also be used for fun and social activities and this is how many people will use it. Aside from the major energy, minor aspects are mixed. Good choices will lead to good times. Bad ones ...

Saturday, 8th

☽	⚼	♇	6:53
☽	△	♃	7:16
♀	D		9:15
☿	⚼	♆	9:25
☽	⚺	☉	3:27PM
☽	☌	♀	4:46
☽	⚻	♅	5:03
♂	△	♆	9:05
☽	#	♇	9:15
☽	☍	♆	11:05
☽	⚹	♂	11:11

Today's biggest news is that Venus turns direct after having backed up in our skies since July . As it picks up speed over the next several days, those who have reignited old flames will start to remember why these went out in the first place. This is not to say that it can't work out, but reasons why not will become more apparent. There are two more major energies today. The first can bring problems to communication and transportation, especially where intoxicants and the otherwise out of it are involved. Watch for spaciness across the board and be especially careful in traffic. The second is much more positive and can be used in many ways, but is likely to be seen as high social energy. Plan for all manner of fun activities. Minor aspects are mixed, but good choices should yield good times.

Sunday, 9th

☽	∠	☿	12:58
☽	#	♆	4:41
☉	⚺	♀	9:18
☽	△	♇	11:07
☉	☍	♅	11:45
☽	//	♄	4:55PM
☽	→	♍	6:10
☽	☌	♄	7:58

High energy from yesterday, both positive and cautionary, will remain with us through today. Reread and apply. There are two more major energies to deal with. The first will shed light on relationships. Things should be seen with clearer eyes than over the past several weeks. Make splits amicable and commitments intentional. The second is a reprise of the contradictory energy from Friday. Have fun, but watch for the crazies and deal very carefully with whatever authority you may encounter. Aside from the major energy, the early predawn is mixed and late Saturday night party people should make good choices. Watch for spaciness in

September 2007   Pacific Time

the late predawn. Good moods should run through the rest of the morning, but be aware that the Moon will be void of course from 11:07 this morning until 6:10 this evening when it enters Virgo. At that point the energy will lift noticeably and general moods will tend to become more discerning and concerned with detail.

Monday, 10th

☽ ∥ ♀	5:23
☽ ⚺ ☿	9:28
♀ ⚻ ♅	10:21
☽ □ ♃	4:45PM
☽ # ♅	7:51

There are two major energies running through today. The first easily brings problems to relationships. Watch for sudden, unrealistic and unreasonable demands for change. If trouble pops up, switch to damage control and minimize the aftershocks. You will notice energy levels rising throughout the day as tomorrow morning's new Moon rolls in. Be sure to make the right kinds of beginnings. Take a communicative approach and go for it through the workday. There may be some exaggerated emotional responses in the late afternoon and erratic irritability in the early to later evening.

Tuesday, 11th

☽ ∥ ☉	1:30
☽ ☍ ♅	2:18
☽ ⚺ ♀	2:28
☽ # ☿	3:50
☉ ⚹ ☽	5:31
☽ ☌ ☉	5:44
☽ ⚻ ♆	8:37
☽ □ ♂	11:31
☉ # ☿	3:31PM
☽ □ ♇	9:14

Today is new Moon day. It is exact at 5:44 this morning. This new Moon is also an eclipse, which serves to intensify its effect. Remember that what you do around new Moon tends to bring results at the next full Moon. Obviously it pays to begin things that you would like to see the results of. With this particular new to full period you will want to be careful in relationships and focus on self-discipline. Avoid general spaciness and overindulgence of recreational substances. There is another major energy today that is very good for looking within and coming to deeper self-understanding. The predawn through the morning is mixed at best and good choices will be needed. Things will open up through the afternoon and early evening, but watch the later evening for coercive irritability. Also be aware that the Moon will be void of course from 9:14 tonight through much of tomorrow's predawn.

Wednesday, 12th

☽ → ♎	4:31
☽ ⚺ ♄	6:59
☽ ⚼ ♀	8:16
☽ # ☉	1:42PM
☽ ⚼ ♆	2:09
☉ ⚻ ♆	5:20
☽ ∥ ☿	6:28
☽ ∥ ♅	10:04

Last night's Moon void of course period runs through much of today's predawn and finally ends at 4:31 when the Moon enters Libra. At that point the energy will lift and general moods will tend to become more concerned with balance and beauty. Consider the new Moon to continue through today and much of tomorrow. There are two more major energies. The first brings out the spacecases in a major way. Watch for the inebriated and otherwise out of it. The second

110   Astro-Weather

Pacific Time   September 2007

is much more positive and is very good for any activity involving communication and transportation. Take a cooperative approach and much may be accomplished. This energy may be taken for fun, but has its serious uses as well. Minor aspects are of little help and the right choices are needed.

Thursday, 13th

☿	⚹	♃	3:43
☽	⚹	♃	4:23
☽	☌	☿	4:28
☽	∠	♄	1:13PM
☽	⚻	♅	1:30
☽	#	♀	2:37
☽	⚹	♀	2:37
☽	△	♆	8:06
☽	⚺	☉	10:32

High energy from yesterday, both cautionary and positive, will continue with us through today. The positive energy will be the stronger of the two. Make good use of it. there is another major energy that is also very good for communication and transportation, especially where electricity and electronic media are involved. Begin new projects along these lines. Aside from the major energy, most of the predawn is open. Take an expansive and communicative approach through the late predawn. The morning to the midday is open. Watch the early afternoon for a period of hard attitudes and erratic emotional responses. Things should turn around rapidly, however, and good moods should be dominant from the mid afternoon through the late night.

Friday, 14th

☿	∥	♅	12:50
☽	#	♄	1:16
☽	△	♂	2:00
☽	⚹	♇	9:10
☽	∠	♃	10:49
☽	∥	♆	3:22PM
☽	—	♏	4:36
☽	⚼	♅	7:38
☽	⚹	♄	7:46
☽	∥	♇	11:19

High energy from the past couple days will continue through today. Use it well. The predawn is mixed. Take a fun and active approach and avoid feelings of restriction and frustration, and hard attitudes. Continue to take an active as well as cooperative approach through the early morning. Get anything important done, however, before 9:10 this morning as the Moon will be void of course from then until 4:36 this afternoon when it enters Scorpio. At that point the energy will lift noticeably and general moods will tend to become more intense. Friday night social energy will take off as the void of course ends. There is a period of mixed energy in the evening. Watch for erratic emotional responses and choose a rather more disciplined and settled approach.

Saturday, 15th

☽	∠	☉	7:33
☽	⚼	♂	9:44
☽	∠	♆	3:32PM
☽	⚺	♃	5:29

Late Friday night social scenes should be largely unimpeded into today's predawn. Take a cooperative approach and take the time to look beneath the surface. The rest of the predawn is open. Watch the early through mid morning for irritability and minor aggression. Most of the afternoon opens up, but the mid afternoon will have a brief period of coercive irritability. This will pass quickly if it is noticed at all and good moods will run from the late afternoon through

Astro-Weather

September 2007   Pacific Time

the late night. Enjoy, but watch for erratic behavior in the very late night as a major energy from tomorrow starts to roll in.

Sunday, 16ᵗʰ

☽ ⚻ ☿	1:07
☽ △ ♅	1:56
☽ □ ♀	4:31
☽ ∥ ♃	4:38
☿ ⚼ ♅	7:59
☽ □ ♆	8:40
☽ ⚼ ♂	11:25
☿ ∠ ♄	1:54PM
☽ ⚹ ☉	4:40
☽ ⚼ ♂	5:31
☽ ⚻ ♇	9:55

There are two major energies running throughout the day, both of which are cautionary. The first easily brings problems to communication and transportation especially where electricity and electronic media are involved. Watch for sudden, erratic challenges. This energy also brings out the nutballs. Watch for erratic and bizarre behavior of all kinds and be especially careful in traffic. The second is related and also brings problems in communication and transportation. This energy easily brings about experiences of restriction and frustration with a tendency to act out on it. These two energies are a bad combination that can result in harsher and longer lasting consequences than usual. Be especially careful in traffic and resist any temptation to escalate. Minor aspects are mixed at best and good choices will be necessary. Also be aware that the Moon will be void of course from 4:40 this afternoon through most of tomorrow's predawn.

Monday, 17ᵗʰ

☽ — ♐	5:20
☽ □ ♄	9:06
☽ ∠ ☿	11:19
☉ □ ♂	1:48PM
☿ ⚹ ♀	2:29

Last night's Moon void of course period runs through most of today's predawn and finally ends at 5:20 this morning when the Moon enters Sagittarius. At that point the energy will lift noticeably and general moods will tend to become more expansive and open to a wide range of ideas. There are two major energies running throughout today. The first is significantly cautionary and begins a several day period that definitely bears watching. This aspect is very high energy, but excessive in its nature. Be very careful in your dealings with authority and in any situation where force and power may be at play. The second is much more positive and is the one to focus on. This energy is very good for communication in relationships, make good use of it. There is no help from minor aspects so choose wisely.

Tuesday, 18ᵗʰ

☽ ☌ ♃	6:33
☽ □ ♅	2:03PM
☽ △ ♀	6:25
☿ △ ♆	7:00
☽ ⚹ ♆	8:43
☽ ⚹ ☿	8:56

The cautionary energy mentioned yesterday remains very much with us through today. It is joined by another major energy that is once again much more positive. This aspect is very good for any activity involving prayer, meditation, and spiritual practices of any kind. Those involved should make good use of this. The predawn is open. Take an expansive

Pacific Time   September 2007

approach through the early morning. There may be a brief period of erratic emotional responses in the early to mid afternoon, but this will pass quickly. Good moods should dominate through the evening and late night.

Wednesday, 19th

☽	☍	♂	8:02
☉	□	♆	8:59
☽	☌	♆	9:43
☽	□	☉	9:46
☽	—	♑	4:51PM
☽	△	♄	9:02

The complex of cautionary energies running through the past several days is aggravated by today's major energy. This aspect easily brings about the exposure of secret and coercive activities up to and including violence. Do not let minor disputes escalate. This energy also easily brings problems with and for authority. Watch for attempts at regime change on many levels. Avoid any temptation to mess with authority figures of any kind and don't get caught in anyone else's crossfire. Minor aspects are of no help through the daytime and there is a period of intensely bad moods through the mid to late morning. Also be aware that the Moon will be void of course from 9:46 this morning until 4:51 this afternoon when the Moon enters Capricorn. At that point the energy will lift and general moods will tend to become more down to earth and concerned with accomplishment.

Thursday, 20th

☽	⚻	♀	12:38
☽	⚼	♆	1:55
☿	#	♀	4:24PM
☽	⚺	♃	5:32
☽	✶	♅	11:53

The high cautionary period continues through today. Reread the past few days and apply. There are two more major energies running through today. The first will stimulate a great deal of communication in relationships. This can go either way and in the context of this cautionary period, great care should be taken. The second is central to this period and is highly cautionary. Watch for all manner of secret and coercive activities up to and including violence. There is a compulsiveness to this energy and people can easily find themselves in dangerous situations before having time to consider. Do not let minor disputes escalate and under no circumstances allow yourself to be drawn into altercations with strangers.

Friday, 21st

♂	☍	♆	1:40
☽	⚻	♄	1:52
☽	⚼	♀	6:02
☽	⚺	♆	6:17
☽	□	☿	12:51PM
♀	☍	♆	1:00
☽	⚺	♆	6:38

The high cautionary energy mentioned yesterday peaks in today's predawn, but will remain with us through today and tomorrow at least. By now this combination of energies will have been noticed and people will be talking about it. This has not been a slow news week. There is another major energy running through the day that is also cautionary. Watch for spaciness and confusion in relationships especial-

Astro-Weather   113

September 2007   Pacific Time

☽ ☍ ♂   7:17
☽ ∠ ♃   9:40
☽ △ ☉   11:13

ly where the inebriated and otherwise out of it are involved. This again is a bad combination as misunderstandings can easily lead to overreactions and very unfortunate results. Count to ten and then do it again. Minor aspects are of very little help through the day and minor irritants can easily blow up out of all proportion. Tread lightly on those eggshells. Moods should become more positive in the very late night, but this is not the most positive, social Friday night you've ever experienced. Also be aware that the Moon will be void of course from 11:13 tonight in to tomorrow's predawn.

Saturday, 22nd

☽ → ♒   1:16
☽ # ♂   1:53
☽ ∠ ♅   3:29
☽ ☍ ♄   5:44
☽ ∥ ♃   8:31
☽ ∠ ♆   9:39PM
☽ ⚼ ♂   11:17

Last night's Moon void of course period ends at 1:16 when the Moon enters Aquarius. At that point the energy will lift and general moods will tend to become more independent and free-thinking. The high cautionary energy from the past few days will linger through today with fallout continuing at the very least. Be kind to those licking wounds. There is scattered minor irritability following the void of course and running through the predawn. Moods will open up through the rest of the day and most of the evening. There may be a brief period of coercive irritability in the later evening to late night. Continue to be careful in social situations.

Sunday, 23rd

☽ ✶ ♃   12:50
☉ → ♎   2:51
☽ ⚼ ☉   4:09
☽ ⚻ ♅   6:06
☿ # ♄   7:55
☽ ∥ ♇   10:31
☽ ☌ ♆   12:07PM
☽ ⚺ ♀   1:50
☽ ∥ ♆   5:19
☽ △ ☿   11:21
☽ ✶ ♇   11:43

The Sun enters the cardinal air sign Libra in today's late predawn. This is the Autumnal Equinox and signals the beginning of the fall harvest season. Results from the projects begun back at the Vernal Equinox should be taking shape and rolling in. Continue to watch for results and fallout from the cautionary period running through last week. There are two more major energies running through today. The first can bring problems to communication and transportation, especially where people run into restriction and frustration. This can result in harsher and longer lasting consequences than usual, so deal carefully with it. The second is very good for seeing beneath the surface, coming to deeper understanding, and making positive changes. Things which are normally kept hidden and go unnoticed will emerge. Observe. Minor aspects are once again of no help and good choices will be necessary.

Monday, 24th

☽ △ ♂   2:13
☿ ✶ ♇   3:55

The positive energy mentioned yesterday will remain with us through today. There is still likely to be fallout and ad-

114   Astro-Weather

☽	∥	☿	5:05
☽	—	♓	5:54
☽	#	♄	7:03
☽	⚻	☉	7:54
☽	☍	♄	10:28
☽	#	♀	12:28PM

justments made from last week's cautionary period. Aside from the major energy, good moods should run through the early predawn. The Moon will be void of course this morning, however, from 2:13 until 5:54 when it enters Pisces. At that point the energy will lift and general moods will tend to become more mellow if a bit spacy. Watch the early morning for hard attitudes and general irritability. The late morning contributes a brief period of more hard attitudes. There may be relationship issues to deal with at the midday, but this is likely to pass quickly and hopefully will not be noticed at all. The rest of the afternoon through the evening and into the late night is open.

Tuesday, 25th

☽	⚼	☿	2:46
☽	∥	♅	3:24
☽	□	♃	4:24
☽	☌	♅	8:43
☽	⚺	♆	2:28PM
☽	⚻	♀	6:00
☽	∥	☉	9:17

There are three major energies coming into focus throughout today. The first is positive for self-discipline, older people, and traditional matters. This energy can be useful in dealing with bosses and other authority figures. The second is more cautionary and easily brings problems to communication and transportation, especially where people attempt to say and do too much. Don't bite off more than you can chew or make promises you may not be able to deliver on. You will notice energy levels rising throughout the day as the third major energy, tomorrow's full Moon, rolls in. Enjoy the high energy but be careful.

Wednesday, 26th

☽	□	♇	1:32
☉	⚺	♄	2:00
☿	∠	♃	2:36
☽	#	☉	5:04
☽	⚻	☿	5:16
☽	□	♂	5:31
☽	—	♈	7:22
☿	△	♂	10:55
☽	⚻	♄	12:06PM
☽	☍	☉	12:44
☽	∠	♆	2:43
☽	⚼	♀	7:09
☽	#	♅	10:19

Today is full Moon day. It is exact at 12:44 this afternoon. Remember that full Moons are always high energy and deserve to be approached with respect. The high positive energy mentioned yesterday is connected to the full Moon and will extend strongly through today and into tomorrow. Make good use of it. On the other hand, you will want to watch for spaciness due to another related aspect coming into effect that is exact tomorrow. Yesterday's cautionary energy will also run through today and bears watching. There is one more major energy today that contradicts the one just mentioned that is very positive for all matters involving communication, transportation, and the uses of energy and power. Avoiding the pitfalls of the cautionary energies, this can be a highly positive go-for-it work day. There will be a Moon void of course period this morning from 5:31 until 7:22 when the Moon enters Aries. At that point the energy will lift and general moods will tend to become more assertive and aggressive. Minor aspects are of no help through the day and good choices will be very important.

Thursday, 27th

☽	△	♃	5:22
☽	⚺	♅	9:00
☿	→	♏	10:19
☽	⚼	♄	12:17PM
☽	∥	♀	12:18
☽	⚹	♆	2:39
☽	∥	♄	5:11
☉	⚼	♆	6:24
☽	△	♀	8:03

Consider the full Moon and attendant energies to run strongly through today and tomorrow at least. There are two more major energies. The first indicates a general shift in attitudes concerning communication and transportation toward a more intense and passionate mode. The second is the spacy energy mentioned yesterday which peaks tonight. The space cases will be out and about and you will want to watch for the inebriated and otherwise out of it. Aside from the major energy, good moods should run through most of the morning. Watch for a downturn at the midday with a brief period of hard attitudes. Take a disciplined approach through the evening. Moods will improve once again in the later evening and through the late night.

Friday, 28th

☽	△	♇	1:34
☽	#	☿	2:56
☽	⚼	♃	5:29
☽	#	♆	6:45
☽	⚹	♂	6:58
☽	→	♉	7:16
☽	☍	☿	8:49
☽	∠	♅	8:50
☿	⚼	♅	8:57
☽	△	♄	12:21PM
☽	#	♇	1:00
☽	⚻	☉	3:56
♂	→	♋	4:54

Full Moon energy will remain with us through much of the day. Respect it. The cautionary spacy energy mentioned yesterday will continue as well. There are two more major energies running through the day. The first easily leads to problems in communication and transportation, especially where electricity, electronic media, and technology are involved. This energy also stimulates erratic and even bizarre behavior. Watch for the crazies who will be out and about, and be especially careful in traffic. The second indicates a general shift in the way energy and power are used toward a more sensitive and protective mode. Good moods should run through the early predawn, but watch the mid predawn for argumentativeness. The morning is mixed. There is a short Moon void of course period this morning from 6:58 until 7:16 when the Moon enters Taurus. At that point the energy will lift and general moods will tend to become more down to earth and concerned with enjoyment. Watch for a brief period of irritability following the void of course. The midday through mid afternoon is mixed and a disciplined approach will serve best. The evening into the late night is open. Have fun but choose well.

Saturday, 29th

☽	⚼	♇	1:31
☽	⚻	♃	5:40
☽	∠	♂	7:42
☽	⚹	♅	8:46
☽	#	♃	1:23PM
☽	□	♆	2:32
☽	⚼	☉	5:43

Late Friday social situations may go south as the predawn progresses. Watch the late predawn to very early morning for erratic and exaggerated emotional responses. The early through mid morning is mixed. Watch for minor aggressiveness and choose instead a friendly and innovative approach. The early to mid afternoon may have more exaggerated emotional responses and spaciness to deal with. The late

Pacific Time   September 2007

☽ ∥ ♂   7:59
☽ □ ♀   10:11

afternoon to very early evening chips in with more minor irritability. Take an active approach in the evening, but watch the late night for relationship issues. Also be aware that the Moon will be void of course from 10:11 tonight through tomorrow's predawn. This may be a Saturday night to pack it in early.

Sunday, 30th

☽ ⚻ ♆   1:45
☽ → ♊   7:34
☽ ⚺ ♂   8:48
☿ ∥ ♆   9:56
☽ ⚻ ☿   12:35PM
☽ □ ♄   1:10
☽ △ ☉   8:01
☿ □ ♄   11:18

Last night's Moon void of course period runs through today's predawn and ends at 7:34 this morning when the Moon enters Gemini. At that point the energy will lift noticeably and general moods will tend to become more communicative. There are two major energies running through the day. The first is positive for making new beginnings in prayer, meditative, and spiritual pursuits. Those involved in these things should make the most of it. The second is related to the first and serves to strengthen and solidify these new beginnings. This energy is also very good for negotiation and coming to long term agreement. Moods will be mixed following the void of course and through the rest of the day. Good moods will run through the evening and into the late night.

Astro-Weather

October 2007

Overview

As October rolls in, the Jupiter square Saturn that came back into focus last month is soon to peak. Intensity will build through the first two weeks and then begin to subside. By the end of the month it will still be with us, but fading fast. This period may well produce moments when it will be tempting to doubt that this will ever end. Do not despair, and know that what is really happening is combatants getting licks in while they still can. Also, since Jupiter is involved, this is all likely to be more noise than actual damage. With Jupiter, any damage will have a significant silver lining, even if it is not very apparent at first. As Jupiter moves away from the square to Saturn through the second half of the month, it moves into a sextile to Neptune that peaks very late in the month. This is very positive and is energy for compromise and acceptance of differences between religions and philosophies. This is the energy to focus on and will be very amenable to any global prayer and meditation for peace efforts. Let us all make the most of this. Please participate however you can.

On the more personal level, October will settle down a little. There is very high but very contradictory energy on the 8th and 9th. The biggest news is that Mercury turns retrograde for the last time this year on the 11th and backs up in our sky until November 1st. See the retrograde pages at the beginning of the book for more on these periods. Read ahead and plan for dealing with the high energy days that we do have, and try not to beat your head against the retrograde wall. The most significant daytime Moon void of course periods will be the 4th, 16th, most notably the 27th, and in the western time zones, the 31st. There are a few half day voids to be aware of as well.

Monday, 1st

☽ ☍ ♃   7:16
☽ ☐ ♅   9:52
☽ ⚹ ☿   3:13PM
☽ △ ♆   3:58

High positive energy from yesterday will continue through today. Make good use of it. Aside from the major energy, the predawn is open. The early morning may have some exaggerated emotional reactions. Watch the late morning for erratic irritability. The early afternoon is open, but the mid to late afternoon is mixed. Avoid an erratic argumentativeness and choose a more friendly attitude with an intuitive approach. The evening through the late night is open once again.

Tuesday, 2nd

☽	□	♀	2:31
☽	☍	♇	3:52
☽	→	♋	9:58
☽	☌	♂	12:55PM
☽	□	♄	4:17
☽	∠	♆	5:43
☽	△	☿	6:38

There is a major energy coming into focus today that can be very positive for taking relationships to deeper levels. There is, however, a strong sexual component to this that needs to be carefully dealt with. Aside from the major energy, the early predawn is open, but the mid predawn is mixed. Take a friendly and cooperative approach, avoiding a coercive irritability. The Moon will be void of course this morning from 3:52 until 9:58 when it enters Cancer. At that point the energy will lift noticeably and general moods will tend to become more sensitive and protective. Take an active and disciplined approach through the afternoon. This gives way to a mixed period. Avoid spaciness and take a friendly, communicative approach instead.

Wednesday, 3rd

☽	□	☉	3:06
☽	∠	♀	6:01
♀	△	♇	6:15
☽	⚻	♃	11:40
☽	△	♅	1:42PM
☽	∠	♄	7:03
☽	⚻	♆	8:17

The positive energy mentioned yesterday for taking relationships to deeper levels peaks this morning and runs strongly through today and into tomorrow. Remember that there is a strong sexual component to this which can be unsettling for some people. Watch the mid predawn to early morning for a period of intensely bad moods and relationship issues. Most of the rest of the morning opens up. The midday may have some exaggerated emotional reactions, but good moods should prevail. Get anything important done, however, before 1:42 this afternoon as the Moon will be void of course from then through much of tomorrow.

Thursday, 4th

☽	⚻	♇	9:02
☽	⚺	♀	10:33
☽	//	♂	1:34PM
☽	∠	♃	3:07
☽	→	♌	3:27
☽	∠	♅	4:49
☽	⚺	♂	8:26
☽	#	♃	9:08
☽	⚺	♄	10:40
☿	//	♇	11:25

Yesterday's long Moon void of course period runs through most of today and finally ends at 3:27 this afternoon when the Moon enters Leo. At that point the energy will lift very noticeably and general moods will tend to become more intense and concerned with self. Try to relax and take it easy through the workday and tend to old business. There is a major energy coming into focus today that is positive for seeing beneath the surface, coming to deeper understanding, and initiating positive change. Remember the void of course, however, and put off beginnings until after it ends. Take an active yet disciplined approach through the evening and late night.

Friday, 5th

☽	□	☿	3:53
☽	∠	♇	12:51PM
☽	□	☉	2:13

Good moods should run through the early predawn, but watch the mid predawn for irritability and argumentativeness. Most of the morning opens up. There may be a brief

October 2007   Pacific Time

| ☽ △ ♃ | 7:24 |
| ☽ ⊼ ♅ | 8:44 |

period of coercive irritability at the midday, but this will pass quickly if it is noticed at all. The rest of the afternoon through the evening turns around and becomes much more positive with good moods dominating. Watch the later evening for a brief period of erratic irritability. Sidestep that and make the right choices to keep the glow going for a more positive, social Friday night.

Saturday, 6th

☽ # ☿	12:39
☽ ∠ ♂	1:28
☽ # ♇	1:57
☽ ☍ ♆	3:47
☽ # ♆	9:21
☽ △ ♇	5:22PM
☽ ∠ ☉	9:12
☽ ☌ ♀	10:29

There is scattered minor irritability through the predawn. Watch for argumentativeness, aggression, a coercive irritability, and spaciness. Late Friday night party people may want to call it early. Most of the morning opens up, but there may be more spaciness in the mid morning. The afternoon becomes open again and good moods should run from the late afternoon through the early evening. Watch for a slight downturn in the late night and be aware of a short Moon void of course period starting at 10:29 tonight running into tomorrow's early predawn.

Sunday, 7th

☽ – ♍	12:03
☽ ∥ ♄	3:26
☽ □ ♂	7:13
☽ ☌ ♄	8:07
☽ ∥ ♀	11:36
☽ □ ☿	3:45PM
♀ – ♍	11:52

Last night's Moon void of course period ends at 12:03 this morning when the Moon enters Virgo. At that point the energy will lift and general moods will tend to become more discerning and concerned with detail. Late Saturday night party people will find a boost in energy as the void of course ends. Take an active yet disciplined approach through the morning. A communicative approach will serve best through the late afternoon. The rest of the evening through most of the late night is open. There is a major energy late tonight that indicates a general shift in relationships and aesthetics toward a more discerning and detailed mode.

Monday, 8th – Columbus Day

☽ # ♅	12:15
☽ # ☉	2:47
☽ ⊻ ☉	4:56
☽ □ ♃	6:02
☽ ☍ ♅	6:30
☽ ⊼ ♆	1:56PM
♂ □ ♄	8:44
☉ □ ♃	9:04
☽ ∠ ☿	10:12
☉ ⊼ ♅	11:48

There are four major energies running throughout the day that are highly contradictory. The first is very positive for the uses of energy and power in very solid and disciplined ways. Much may be accomplished. The second is high positive itself. Many will be feeling confident and good about themselves with a strong sense of wellbeing. Problems can set in where people get carried away. The third is somewhat related yet brings out the crazies. Watch for erratic and bizarre behavior of all kinds and be very careful around authority, which can turn on you in a second. The fourth is even more cautionary. Be very careful around water and

♂	∠	♆	12:27
☽	□	♇	4:08
☽	–	♎	10:57
♃	□	♅	11:23
☽	⌣	♀	1:26PM
☉	//	♅	5:58
☽	∠	♆	7:41
☽	⌣	♄	7:47
☽	□	♂	8:21
☉	∠	♀	11:45

☽	⌣	☿	4:45
☽	//	♅	6:20
☽	//	☉	7:14
☽	#	♀	5:06PM
☽	⊼	♅	6:04
☽	□	♃	6:35
☽	∠	♀	9:40
☽	☌	☉	10:00

☽	△	♆	1:45
☽	∠	♄	2:09
☽	#	♄	3:09
☽	□	♇	4:22PM
☿	℞		9:01
☽	//	♆	11:02
☽	–	♏	11:13

caustic liquids and gases. This also easily leads to a spacy and intoxicant-fueled violence. Minor aspects are of little to no help and good choices will be very important.

Tuesday, 9th

High energy from yesterday, both positive and otherwise, will remain very much with us through today. Reread and apply carefully. There are three more major energies today. The first is a long range outer planet aspect that heats up the ongoing conflict in the international arena. Watch the news as headlines are likely to be generated. The second can bring out the crazies and stimulate erratic behavior. Be careful around authority. On the other hand, it can be positive for beginning projects involving the use of technology and magic. The third sheds light on relationships, but not necessarily in a positive way. The Moon will be void of course this morning from 4:08 until 10:57 when it enters Libra. At that point the energy will lift noticeably and general moods will tend to become more concerned with balance and beauty. Minor aspects are mixed through the afternoon and night time. Good moods are available with the right choices.

Wednesday, 10th

High energy from the last couple of days will remain with us through today, especially the relationship segment. Today and tomorrow together will be new Moon day. It is exact at 10:00 tonight. Remember that what you start at new Moon brings results at the next full Moon. It always pays to start things you want to see the results of at this time. During this new to full Moon period, it will be a good idea to concentrate on relationships and matters involving self-discipline. Most of the predawn is open. Good moods should run through the late predawn. Go for it through the work day. The late afternoon into the late night is mixed, but good moods are available with the right choices. Remember the new Moon and make them.

Thursday, 11th

Consider the new Moon to run strongly through today and tomorrow. Make the right choices and start the right things. Today's other big news, however, is that Mercury turns retrograde late tonight and backs up in our sky until November 1st. During Mercury retrogrades, all things having to do with communication and transportation are prone to snafu and breakdown. Plan extra time for everything; watch for all manner of misunderstandings; avoid the signing of contracts and legal documents; and don't open new businesses. See the retrograde pages at the beginning of this book for more on these periods. Most of today's workday is open to do with as you will, but be aware that the Moon will be void of course from 4:22 this afternoon until 11:13 tonight when the Moon enters Scorpio. At that point the energy will lift and general moods will tend to become more intense.

Friday, 12th

☽	∠	♅	12:14
☽	∠	♃	1:16
☽	□	♀	6:13
☽	∥	♆	7:00
☽	□	♄	8:43
☽	△	♂	10:43
☽	∥	☿	11:30
☽	☌	☿	5:30PM
☉	△	♆	6:39
☽	∠	♇	10:46

There are two major energies coming into focus throughout the day. The first is excellent for any prayer, meditation, or spiritual practices one may be involved in. Be open to the intuitive process and follow guidance. This energy can also be used socially, however, and this is how many people will approach it. The second is rather more cautionary. Watch for people to run into restriction and frustration, with some tendency to act out on it. Pay particular attention to your self-discipline. This energy also easily brings problems with and for authority. Don't smart off to the boss or any other authority figures and don't get caught up in anyone else's foolishness. Minor aspects are mixed, but good moods should prevail. Make the right choices and get a lot done. Have fun tonight, but remember the new Moon and be good.

Saturday, 13th

☉	∠	♄	5:13
☽	△	♅	6:32
☽	⚻	♃	8:05
☽	□	♆	2:23PM
☽	∥	♃	3:24
☽	⚻	☉	4:12
☽	∠	♂	6:03
♀	☌	♄	9:27

High energy from yesterday, both positive and otherwise, will linger through today. Be especially mindful of the more cautionary one as it peaks early this morning and remains active a while longer. There is another major energy that can be positive for making new beginnings, and strengthening and solidifying relationships. This has to be a two way street, however; avoid any impulse to try to impose this where it may not be mutually agreeable. Make a positive gesture in an appropriate situation. Moods should be positive through the morning and early afternoon. Watch for spaciness in the late afternoon and be aware that the Moon will be void of course from 2:23 this afternoon through most of tomorrow morning. Relax, take it easy, and try to have fun tonight, but heed the cautions.

Sunday, 14th

☽	#	♂	12:00
☽	⚻	♆	5:12
☉	#	♀	11:46
☽	—	♐	11:58

There is a major energy running through the day that sheds light on relationships and aesthetic issues. Keep in mind, however, that yesterday's long Moon void of course period runs through the predawn and morning and finally ends at

Pacific Time   October 2007

| ☽ □ ♄ | 9:58PM |
| ☽ □ ♀ | 11:40 |

11:58 this morning when the Moon enters Sagittarius. At that point the energy will lift very noticeably and general moods will tend to become more expansive and open to a wide range of ideas. Relax and take it easy through the void of course, but be prepared for a rush of energy as it ends. Plan some sort of fun activity through the rest of the afternoon and evening. Watch the later, however, for hard attitudes and relationship issues.

Monday, 15th

☽ ⚼ ☉	1:17
☽ ⚻ ♂	1:18
☽ ⚺ ☿	4:50
☽ □ ♅	6:57PM
☽ ☌ ♃	9:31

There is scattered irritability through today's early predawn. Watch for relationship issues followed by just general irritability and erratic aggression. Moods should improve in the late predawn. The workday is open to do with as you will. Make good use of it. Watch the early evening for a period of minor erratic irritability, but good moods should return through the late night.

Tuesday, 16th

☽ □ ♆	2:49
☽ ⚼ ☿	9:36
☿ ∥ ♆	9:59
☽ □ ☉	10:04
♀ □ ♂	10:35
☽ ☌ ♇	5:32PM
☿ □ ♀	8:14

There are four major energies running through the day. The first is positive for seeing beneath the surface and initiating positive change. Things normally kept secret and hidden will be more accessible. The second is very positive for relationships, especially of the male-female variety. The third is also positive for communication in relationships. Remember, however, that Mercury is retrograde and this may be a good time to clear up issues from the past. On the other hand it may be wiser to let sleeping dogs lie. Choose wisely in this matter. The fourth is also positive for any activity involving communication, transportation, and the uses of energy and power. Again, remember the retrograde and focus on dealing with past issues. Get anything important done before 5:32 this afternoon as the Moon will be void of course from then into tomorrow's predawn.

Wednesday, 17th

☽ → ♑	12:02
☿ △ ♂	1:31
☽ ⚼ ♆	8:30
☽ △ ♄	10:16
☽ □ ☿	1:37PM
☽ ☍ ♂	2:42
☽ △ ♀	4:06

Yesterday's Moon void of course period ends at 12:02 this morning when the Moon enters Capricorn. At that point the energy will lift and general moods will tend to become more down to earth and concerned with accomplishment. High positive energy from yesterday will tend to remain with us through today. Reread and make good use of it. The predawn following the void of course is open. Watch the early to mid morning for a brief period of spaciness. Take a disciplined and communicative approach from the late morning through midday. There may be some aggressive-

Astro-Weather   123

October 2007   Pacific Time

ness in the mid afternoon, but this should be easily dealt with and good moods are accessible right on through the evening and late night.

Thursday, 18th

☽	□	♅	5:57
☽	⚺	♃	9:23
☽	⚺	♆	1:35PM
☽	∠	♄	3:33
☽	∠	♀	11:13

Today's predawn is open. Take a friendly and innovative approach through the very early morning. Good moods should continue through most of the work day. The late morning is expansive and communicative. Be open to the intuitive process in the early afternoon. There may be some people opting for minor hard attitudes in the mid afternoon, but this energy will be short lived. The evening is open, but watch the very late night for a downturn.

Friday, 19th

☽	□	☉	1:31
☽	⚺	♇	3:46
☽	#	♂	5:39
☿	□	♄	6:51
☽	—	♒	9:50
☽	∠	♅	10:22
☽	//	♃	1:08PM
☽	∠	♃	2:11
☿	//	♆	5:31
☽	□	☿	6:54
☽	⚼	♄	7:57

There are three major energies active today. The first is normally very positive for any activity involving communication and transportation. It is also excellent for negotiation and coming to long term agreement. Remember, however, that Mercury is retrograde and you will want to primarily deal with issues from the past. The second is very positive for initiating projects involving prayer, meditation, and other spiritual pursuits. Be open to the intuitive process and listen for the still small voice. With Mercury in retrograde, there will be lessons from the past to learn. The third peaks tomorrow morning and sheds light on things normally kept secret and hidden, but in a more positive way than usual. Look within and come to deeper self understanding. The Moon will be void of course this morning from 1:31 until 9:50 when it enters Aquarius. At that point the energy will lift noticeably and general moods will tend to become more independent and free thinking. This will be a high energy social Friday night, but there is scattered minor irritability in the later evening to late night so make good choices.

Saturday, 20th

☽	⚼	♂	1:05
☽	⚼	♀	5:18
☉	□	♇	6:39
☽	∠	♇	7:36
☽	⚺	♅	1:53PM
☽	□	♃	6:00
☽	//	♆	6:52
☽	☌	♆	9:07

High energy from yesterday will remain very much with us through today. Make good use of the energy for greater self understanding and make positive changes. Watch today's early predawn for an erratic aggressiveness. The late predawn may bring relationship issues and the early morning contributes a coercive irritability. Moods will improve through the afternoon and evening. Take an innovative and expansive approach. This is likely to be a high energy social Saturday night. Have a great time.

Pacific Time   October 2007

☽	∥	♆	1:58
☽	⊥	♂	4:45
☽	∥	☿	6:15
☽	□	♇	10:26
☉	#	♄	12:31PM
☽	△	☉	12:34
☽	−	♓	4:01
☿	⊥	♃	4:31
♀	#	♅	6:30
☽	∥	☉	8:11
☽	△	☿	8:22
☽	#	♄	8:40

Sunday, 21st

There are three major energies running through today. The first can bring problems with matters involving self discipline, authority, older people, and traditional matters. Watch for people running into restriction and frustration and acting out on it. Deal carefully with authority figures of all kinds and don't get caught up in anyone else's troubles. Problems produced by this energy can be harsher and longer lasting than normal. The second stimulates a great deal of activity in communication and transportation. Watch for some people to try to say and do too much. Don't bite off more than you can chew, or make promises that will be difficult to deliver. Also watch for problems from the past to recur. The third easily brings problems to relationships. Watch for sudden unreasonable and unrealistic demands for change. Damage control. This energy can also be highly social, but it is erratic, to say the least, and needs to be handled carefully. The Moon will be void of course this afternoon from 12:34 until 4:01 when it enters Pisces. At that point the energy will lift and general moods will become more mellow if a bit spacy. Minor aspects are mixed. Choose well.

☽	☍	♄	1:46
☽	△	♂	7:17
☽	∥	♅	12:27PM
☽	#	♀	1:13
☽	☍	♀	1:48
☽	⊥	☉	4:15
☽	☌	♅	5:58
☽	⊥	☿	7:48
☽	□	♃	10:31

Monday, 22nd

Today's early predawn is open, but watch the mid to late predawn for a brief period of hard attitudes. The rest of the predawn through early morning is open. Take an active and friendly approach through the morning and get a lot done. There may be erratic emotional responses and relationship issues in the afternoon. Deal carefully with this. Try to take a fun and innovative approach through the evening, but watch for some people to fall prey to minor irritability later. The late night is mixed. Watch for exaggerated emotional responses followed by better moods into tomorrow's predawn.

☽	⚺	♆	12:45
☉	−	♏	12:15PM
☽	□	♇	1:15
☉	⊥	♅	4:30
☉	☌	☿	4:54
☿	⊥	♅	5:14
☽	−	♈	6:23
☽	⚻	☿	6:33
☽	⚻	☉	6:50
☿	−	♎	8:37

Tuesday, 23rd

There are five major energies running through the day. The first is the Sun's entry into the fixed water sign Scorpio. During this time, continue to gather and store the harvest from the projects begun back at the Vernal Equinox. The second brings out the crazies. Watch for all manner of bizarre and erratic behavior. If you see someone whose cheese seems to have slipped off their cracker, it is very likely so. The third is good for introspection and coming to greater self understanding. Learn from the past. The fourth is related to the second and pulls communication and transporta-

October 2007   Pacific Time

tion into the problem area. Watch for all kinds of trouble involving electricity, electronic media, and technology. Be very careful in traffic. The fifth, which occurs late tonight, indicates a general shift in communication and transportation towards a more balanced mode. This is by retrograde motion, however, so continue to pay attention to issues from the past. Be aware that the Moon will be void of course from 1:15 this afternoon until 6:23 this evening when it enters Aries. At that point the energy will lift noticeably and general moods will tend to become somewhat more assertive and aggressive. Minor aspects are mixed at best and this will be a day for very good choices.

Wednesday, 24th

☽	⋌	♆	1:17
☽	⊼	♄	3:49
☿	⋌	♀	7:58
☽	∥	♀	8:01
☽	□	♂	9:36
☽	#	♅	10:27
☉	∥	☿	2:36PM
☽	⊼	♀	6:11
☽	⋎	♅	6:42
☽	△	♃	11:42

High energy from yesterday will remain with us through today and is joined by three more major energies. The first easily stimulates relationship issues. There is likely to be a great deal of communication in this area, but watch for things from the past to reappear. This may or (more likely) may not be good. Choose wisely what you say and how you respond. The second is good for introspection and coming to greater self understanding. Again, learn from the past. The third, which peaks in tomorrow's predawn, is a continuation and strengthening of the erratic relationship energy mentioned last Sunday. Reread and apply those cautions strongly today and through the next two or three days. Minor aspects are of no help through the day and early evening, but moods may improve later.

Thursday, 25th

☽	∥	♄	12:48
☽	□	♆	1:12
♀	☍	♅	2:07
☽	#	☿	3:36
☽	⋌	♄	3:50
☽	#	☉	5:52
☽	△	♆	1:15PM
☽	☍	☿	2:45
☽	#	♆	6:03
☽	–	♉	6:06
☽	⋌	♅	6:18
☽	⋌	♀	7:26
☽	☍	☉	9:51
☽	⋌	♃	11:35

Reread and apply carefully all the cautions from the past few days. Today is full Moon day. It is exact at 9:51 tonight. Remember that full Moons are always high energy and deserve to be approached with respect. This particular full Moon has both positive and cautionary energy surrounding it. Today's early predawn should be good mood oriented. Watch the mid predawn for a downturn with minor irritability and hard attitudes that will likely run through the late predawn. Much of the workday is open. The early to mid afternoon is mixed, however, and a cooperative approach will yield more positive results. The Moon will be void of course from 2:45 this afternoon until 6:06 this evening when it enters Taurus. At that point the energy will lift noticeably and general moods will tend to become more down to earth and concerned with enjoyment. There is more scattered minor irritability following the void of

126   Astro-Weather

Pacific Time   October 2007

☽	#	♇	12:31
☽	△	♄	3:31
☿	#	♄	6:28
☽	□	♂	9:41
☿	□	♇	10:56
☽	⊾	♇	12:47PM
☽	□	♅	5:45
☽	△	♀	8:31
☽	⊼	♃	11:22

☽	□	♆	12:15
☽	#	♃	2:47
☉	⊾	♃	6:32
☽	∥	♂	9:33
☽	⊾	♂	9:35
☽	⊼	☿	10:45
☽	⊼	♇	12:22PM
☽	–	♊	5:11

☽	⊼	☉	12:19
☽	□	♄	3:01
☽	⊾	☿	9:18
☽	⊻	♂	9:48
☽	□	♅	5:16PM
☽	□	♀	11:41
☽	☍	♃	11:49

course and you will want to make good choices. Enjoy the high intensity, but choose well.

Friday, 26th

Consider the full Moon to run through today and tomorrow at least. There are two more major energies running through today. The first can bring problems to communication and transportation, especially where people run into restriction and frustration. Watch for some people to have promised more than they can deliver. Be very careful in traffic. The second is very good for seeing beneath the surface and making positive changes. Things normally kept secret and hidden will be much more available, but in a more positive way than at other times. Remember, however, that Mercury is retrograde and it's probably a good idea to focus on issues from the past. Minor aspects are mixed through the day and into the late night, but with good choices, good moods will be available. Have fun tonight, but guard against getting carried away.

Saturday, 27th

There is a major energy running through the day that tends to have people feeling positive and good about themselves. Problems pop up because it is so easy to get carried away with this energy. Watch for all manner of overindulgence and excess. Late Friday night social scenes are likely to be highly energized into today's predawn, but you will want to watch for exaggerated emotional responses and spaciness. Also be aware that the Moon will be void of course from 12:15 this morning until 5:11 this afternoon when the Moon enters Gemini. At that point the energy will lift very noticeably and general moods will tend to become more communicative. This will be a day to relax, lay low, and tend to old business if any business at all. There will be a big boost in social energy as the void of course ends.

Sunday, 28th

There are two major energies coming into focus today. They can both be viewed as highly social, but are cautionary as well. The first easily leads to overindulgence of all kinds and people will be proving, once again, that it's possible to get too much of a good thing. The second often brings about spaciness and confusion in relationships, especially where recreational substances are overdone and the otherwise out of it are involved. If trouble pops up, switch to damage control and ride it out. Minor aspects are of little

Astro-Weather

October 2007   Pacific Time

help, and good choices will be needed.

Monday, 29th

☽	△	♆	12:06
♀	□	♃	2:08
☽	⊿	☉	2:15
♀	⊼	♆	5:47
☽	△	☿	8:34
☽	☍	♇	12:51PM
☽	—	♋	5:49
☉	□	♄	8:41
♃	□	♆	8:58

The high social energy mentioned yesterday will remain very much with us today. Some will be tempted to a three day weekend, but this is probably not a good idea. You will, in fact, want to pass on the overblown social energy in favor of today's other energy. There are two more major energies running through the day. The first is very positive for dealing with things involving self-discipline, authority, older people, and traditional matters. With a disciplined approach, much may be accomplished. Remember that Mercury is retrograde, however, and focus on old business. The second is a long range outer planet aspect that should indicate positive news in the ongoing international conflict. Be sure to work around the Moon void of course this afternoon that runs from 12:51 until 5:49 when the Moon enters Cancer. At that point the energy will lift and general moods will tend to become more sensitive and protective.

Tuesday, 30th

☽	⊿	♆	12:58
☽	□	♄	4:31
☽	△	☉	5:04
☽	☌	♂	12:12PM
☽	△	♅	7:22

High energy from yesterday, especially the positive variety, will remain with us through today. Reread and make good use of it. There may be minor spaciness in the early predawn, but this will pass quickly if it's noticed at all. Good moods should run strongly from the late predawn through the early morning. Go for it through the workday with an active approach. Moods should be positive through the evening and nighttime. Have a fun and innovative attitude.

Wednesday, 31st – Halloween

☽	⊼	♆	2:44
☽	⊼	♃	3:09
☽	□	♀	6:19
☽	⊿	♄	6:35
☽	□	☿	10:14
♆	D		1:07PM
☽	∥	♂	3:28
☽	⊼	♇	4:32
☽	—	♌	9:49
☽	⊿	♅	9:49
☽	#	♃	11:01

Today's early predawn is open. Watch the mid predawn for erratic spaciness and exaggerated emotional reactions. Moods will be mixed through the morning. Take a friendly and cooperative approach, avoiding any tendency toward hard attitudes. The late morning contributes a period of argumentativeness. Be aware that the Moon will be void of course from 10:14 this morning until 9:49 tonight when it enters Leo. At that point the energy will lift noticeably and general moods will tend to become more intense and concerned with self. This won't be the most positive trick or treating night in memory, but make good choices to get the most out of it that you can.

November 2007

Overview

As November opens, the Jupiter sextile Neptune is still very tight and active. This will be a positive period of rapprochement between religions and philosophies, and between different factions of religions. Rodney King's great question will, for a time at least, seem to be answerable with a yes. Real progress should be seen to be happening even as die-hard warriors of all kinds struggle to keep things going. Even better news is that as Jupiter separates from the sextile to Neptune through the month, it will move on to conjunct Pluto. This aspect will build through the end of this month and peak through the middle of next month. This is a tremendous period of potential positive change, from the international level all the way down to the personal. It will remain very important to participate in any and all prayer and meditation for peace events. We must make the best possible use of this energy.

On the more personal levels, last month's Mercury retrograde ends on the 1st. Give it several days to pick up speed and leave the shadow, but problems with communication and transportation will begin to clear up. A much bigger fly in the ointment is Mars turning Retrograde on the 15th. It will back up until January 30th in 2008. Once again, see the retrograde pages at the beginning of the book for more on these periods. The 19th is a very high energy, but very tricky day that needs to be handled very delicately. This can begin a period that runs into the 22nd for some people and even through the full Moon for the really unfortunate. Read ahead and plan for dealing with this and the other high energy days through the month. The most significant daytime Moon void of course periods are on the 10th and the 15th with a few half day voids to work around as well.

Thursday, 1st

☽	∠	♃	6:21
☽	⚺	♄	9:41
☽	∠	♀	11:31
☽	□	☉	2:19PM
☿	D		3:59
☽	⚺	♂	6:22
☽	∠	♇	7:54

Today's biggest news is that Mercury goes direct late this afternoon after having backed up in our skies since October 11th. As it picks up speed over the next few days, most of the problems we've been having with communication and transportation will begin to clear up. See the retrograde pages at the beginning of the book for more on these periods. Take an expansive approach through the predawn. A disciplined attitude will serve best through much of the morning. Watch the midday through the afternoon for relationship issues followed by a period of intensely bad moods. Moods will be mixed later and good choices are needed.

Friday, 2nd

☽	⚻	♅	1:16
☽	#	♇	6:16
☿	⚺	♀	7:32
☽	☍	♆	9:17
☽	△	♃	10:36
☽	#	♆	2:03PM
☽	#	☉	4:14
☽	□	☿	5:14
☽	⚺	♀	5:59
☽	∠	♂	10:59

There is a major energy running throughout the day that is positive for communication in relationships. Seek to find greater balance by paying attention to the details involved. Watch the early predawn for a brief period of minor erratic irritability. The very early morning may have some coercive attitudes to deal with. The midday is mixed. Opt for the good moods and pass on the spaciness. There may be a recurrence of spaciness in the early to mid afternoon, but moods will improve through the evening. Take a communicative, friendly approach and focus on relationships. There may be a brief downturn in the late night with minor aggressiveness, but this should be easily dealt with. Have fun tonight.

Saturday, 3rd

☽	△	♇	12:14
☽	–	♍	5:44
☽	//	♄	12:11PM
☽	☌	♄	6:46
☽	∠	☿	10:53
☽	#	☿	11:56

There are two major energies coming into focus throughout today. The first is very good for initiating projects involving prayer, meditation, and other spiritual pursuits. The second sheds light on the uses of energy and power. This aspect is very positive for any activity one may be involved in. Generally go for it. The Moon will be void of course this morning from 12:14 until 5:44 when it enters Virgo. At that point the energy will lift and general moods will tend to become more discerning and concerned with detail. Take a disciplined approach through the daytime and on through the evening. There may be a downturn in the late night, but this is again minor and should be easily dealt with.

Sunday, 4th – Daylight Savings Ends

☉	//	♆	2:38
☽	#	♅	3:16
☉	△	♂	3:18
☽	□	♂	3:23
☽	□	☉	3:24
☽	☍	♅	9:51
☉	∠	♇	3:44PM
☽	⚻	♆	6:23
☽	□	♃	8:44
☽	//	♀	9:47

The high energy mentioned yesterday will remain very much with us through today. Continue to pay attention to whatever spiritual practices you may be involved in. Be open to the intuitive process and follow guidance. Also continue to use the high positive energy from yesterday. It will be possible to get a great deal more done than usual. There is another major energy, however, that is more cautionary. This aspect easiiy leads to the exposure of things normally kept secret and hidden. Guard your secrets and observe as others' are exposed. This energy also easily brings problems with and for authority. Keep an eye on motives, yours and others'.

☽	⚺	☿	4:46
☽	☌	♀	9:04
☽	□	♇	10:10
☽	∠	☉	11:48
☽	→	♎	3:47PM
☽	#	♀	3:58
♀	□	♇	10:00

Monday, 5th

There is a major energy coming into focus throughout today that easily leads to a heavy and potentially coercive sexuality. While this may be fun for some, it can be quite unsettling and even dangerous for others. As always with this energy, protect the vulnerable. Today's predawn is open. Take a communicative approach. Get anything important done before 10:10 this morning as the Moon will be void of course from then until 3:47 this afternoon when it enters Libra. At that point the energy will lift and general moods will tend to become more concerned with balance and beauty. Relationship issues are likely throughout the day. Remember the cautionary energy.

☽	∠	♆	12:19
☽	⚺	♄	5:39
☽	//	♅	12:03PM
☽	□	♂	3:51
☽	//	☿	5:09
☽	⚺	☉	8:43
☽	⚻	♅	9:45

Tuesday, 6th

Cautionary energy from yesterday will remain very much with us through today. Reread and apply. There may be a brief period of spaciness in the early predawn, but this will pass quickly if it's noticed at all. Take a disciplined and communicative approach through the early morning. Be open to innovation through the work day, but watch the mid through late afternoon to for potential minor aggression. A communicative approach will serve best through the evening. Maintain a friendly attitude through the late night, but watch for some minor erratic irritability.

☽	#	♄	4:15
☽	△	♆	6:34
☉	△	♅	8:48
☽	□	♃	10:00
☽	∠	♄	12:07PM
☽	☌	☿	9:24
☽	□	♇	10:46

Wednesday, 7th

There is a major energy running through the day that is very positive for anything involving electricity, technology, and magic. Be open to innovation and positive changes of all kinds. Expect the unexpected. Authority may be more approachable and amenable to new ideas than usual. Most of today's predawn is open, but watch the late predawn for potential minor hard attitudes. Good moods will follow and run through the mid morning at least. Hard attitudes will make an attempted comeback at the midday, but this will be fleeting and should be easily dealt with. Have fun today, but be aware that the Moon will be void of course from 10:46 tonight through most of tomorrow's predawn.

☽	⚺	♀	3:25
☽	∠	♅	4:03
☽	//	♆	4:10
☽	→	♏	4:18
☽	//	☉	10:56

Thursday, 8th

Last night's Moon void of course period runs through most of the predawn and ends at 4:18 when the Moon enters Scorpio. At that point the energy will lift and general moods will tend to become more intense. High positive energy from yesterday will continue through today. Make good use

November 2007   Pacific Time

☽	∥	♇	12:52PM
♀	→	♎	1:04
☿	□	♇	2:24
☽	⚹	♃	4:54
☽	□	♄	6:40

of it. There are three more major energies. The first indicates a general shift in relationships and aesthetic matters toward a more balanced and beautiful mode. This is Venus entering its own sign Libra. The second is very positive for looking beneath the surface and coming to greater understanding. Things normally kept secret and hidden will be more accessible than usual. Make positive changes. You will notice energy levels rising throughout the day as the third energy, tomorrow's new Moon, rolls in. It is exact tomorrow afternoon making today, tomorrow and Saturday effectively the new Moon period. Make the right choices and start the right things.

Friday, 9th

☽	△	♂	5:02
☽	⚹	♇	5:13
☽	△	♅	10:24
☽	⚹	♀	12:49PM
☽	☌	☉	3:03
☉	∥	♇	6:39
☽	□	♆	7:19
☽	⚻	♃	11:48

Today is new Moon day. It is exact at 3:03 this afternoon. Remember that what you start at new moon brings results at the next full Moon. During this particular new to full period, you will want to focus on positive personal changes and relationships. There is another major energy running through the day that once again sheds light on things normally kept behind the scenes. This may be rather more personal, however, and you will want to plumb your own depths. Minor aspects are mixed, but with the right choices good moods will be available. Watch the evening for spaciness and be aware that the Moon will be void of course from 7:19 tonight through much of tomorrow.

Saturday, 10th

☽	∥	♃	12:26
☽	#	♂	10:44
☽	⚹	♂	11:32
☽	⚻	♇	11:36
☽	⚻	☿	4:07PM
☽	→	♐	4:58
☿	⚹	♅	9:36
☽	□	♀	10:07

Consider the new Moon to run through today and much of tomorrow. Last night's Moon void of course period runs through most of the daytime and finally ends at 4:58 this afternoon when the Moon enters Sagittarius. At that point the energy will lift very noticeably and general moods will tend to become more expansive and open to a wide range of ideas. Try to relax and take it easy through the void of course, but be prepared for a big rush of energy as it ends and the new Moon energy becomes more active. There is another major energy that is more cautionary. Watch for problems with communication and transportation, especially where electricity, electronic media, technology, and just plain erratic behavior are involved. This will be a very high energy social Saturday night. Have fun, but be careful, especially in traffic.

Sunday, 11th – Veterans' Day

| ☿ | → | ♏ | 12:38 |

High energy from the past couple of days will remain very

Pacific Time   November 2007

☽ □ ♄	7:36
☉ □ ♆	5:41PM
☽ ⊼ ♂	5:51
☽ □ ♅	10:47

much with us through today and is joined by two more major energies. The first indicates a general shift in thinking and communication patterns toward a more intense and, in some cases, secretive mode. The second is highly cautionary and easily brings about a great deal of spaciness. Watch for the inebriated and otherwise out of it who will be very much among us. This energy also confuses authority issues and you will want to be very careful in dealing with these matters. Minor aspects are of no help and good choices will be needed.

Monday, 12th - Veterans' Day (obs.)

☽ ⚹ ☿	1:43
☽ □ ♆	7:41
☽ ⚻ ☉	8:57
♀ ⚹ ♆	12:25PM
☽ ☌ ♃	1:09
☿ # ♄	5:57
☽ ☌ ♇	11:52

The high spacy energy mentioned yesterday will linger through today. Be aware of and compensate for it. There are two more major energies. The first is similar and brings confusion to relationships. Watch for misunderstandings and avoid rushing to judgment as more evidence will be needed. The second can bring problems to communication and transportation, especially where people run into restriction and frustration with a tendency to act out. This energy can be positive for negotiation and coming to long-term agreement, but it needs to be handled carefully. Minor aspects are mixed, but with the right choices, good moods should be available. Be aware that the Moon will void of course from 11:52 tonight through most of tomorrow's predawn.

Tuesday, 13th

☽ → ♑	5:00
☽ □ ☿	11:11
☽ ⚹ ♆	1:29PM
☽ □ ♀	3:57
☽ ⚹ ☉	5:25
☽ △ ♄	7:40

Last night's Moon void of course period runs most of the way through the predawn and ends at 5:00 when the Moon enters Capricorn. At that point the energy will lift and general moods will tend to become more down-to-earth and concerned with accomplishment. Relax and take it easy through the void of course. Take a communicative approach through the morning to midday. Watch the afternoon for spaciness, relationship issues, and general minor irritability. Moods should improve through the evening into the late night. Choose well.

Wednesday, 14th

☽ ☍ ♂	5:31
☽ □ ♅	10:08
☽ ⚻ ♆	6:53PM
☉ ⚻ ♃	11:11

There is a major energy coming into focus throughout the day that is highly positive. People will tend to feel confident and good about themselves. The only problem with this energy is a tendency to get carried away and overindulge. Most of today's predawn is open. There may be some aggressiveness in the late predawn, but this will pass. Good

November 2007   Pacific Time

moods should run through the morning all the way on into the late night. Have a good time, but keep a grip.

Thursday, 15ᵗʰ

♂ ℞	12:25
☽ ∠ ♄	1:05
☽ ⚻ ♃	1:10
☽ □ ☉	1:18
☽ # ♂	3:42
☽ ⚻ ♇	10:41
♀ ⚻ ♄	11:27
☽ ∥ ♃	2:21PM
☽ ∠ ⛢	3:07
☽ → ♒	3:29

The high positive energy from yesterday will remain very much with us through today. Be aware, however, that the Moon will be void of course from 1:18 this morning until 3:29 this afternoon when it enters Aquarius. At that point the energy will lift very noticeably and general moods will tend to become more independent and free thinking. There are two more major energies to be aware of today. The first is Mars turning retrograde in today's early predawn and backing up in our sky until January 30ᵗʰ. During a Mars retrograde, there is somewhat less energy available. Patterns from the past have a tendency to reassert themselves and old disputes easily reignite. It is not the time to initiate things involving the use of energy, power, or force. The second is positive for strengthening and solidifying relationships. Take a communicative approach and make a positive gesture in an appropriate situation. Remember the void of course, and consider that it may be best to wait until it ends to make your move. Relax and take it easy through the void of course and tend to old business, but be prepared for a big rush of energy as it ends.

Friday, 16ᵗʰ

☽ □ ☿	4:42
☽ ⚻ ♄	5:52
☽ ∠ ♃	6:18
☽ △ ♀	7:31
☽ ∥ ☉	2:43PM
☽ ⚻ ♂	2:59
☽ ∠ ♇	3:10
☿ □ ♄	3:21
☽ ⚻ ⛢	7:23
☿ ∠ ♃	8:56
☽ ∥ ♇	11:33

High energy from yesterday will tend to linger through today. Make good use of the positive. There are two more major energies to deal with today. The first is very positive for any activities involving communication and transportation, especially where things are handled in a disciplined manner. This energy is also excellent for negotiation and coming to long term agreement. Seek balance and fairness for all sides. The second is related to the first and exaggerates its effects. This can go either way. It can enhance the previous energy, bringing more benefit, or it can lead to excess and recklessness. Don't bite off more than you can chew or make promises that will be too difficult to deliver. Minor aspects are mixed throughout the day and evening. Good moods will be available to those making the right choices. This will be a high energy social Friday night, but remember the caution.

Saturday, 17ᵗʰ

| ☽ ☌ ♇ | 3:47 |
| ☽ ∥ ♇ | 7:41 |

Late Friday night social scenes are likely to be highly energized well into today's predawn. Take an intuitive approach

☽	□	♃	10:37
☽	∠	♀	1:55PM
☽	□	☉	2:31
☽	//	☿	6:26
☽	∠	♂	6:31
☽	□	♇	6:50
☽	–	♓	11:13

through the late predawn and much of the morning. Be open to guidance from the still small voice within. Good moods should run from the late predawn through the morning. Watch for a downturn, however, through the afternoon with relationship issues and a period of just plain rotten moods. Take a communicative and cooperative approach through the evening, but watch for some minor aggressiveness. The right choices can result in good moods, but be aware that the Moon will be void of course tonight from 6:50 until 11:13 when the Moon enters Pisces. At that point the energy will lift and general moods will tend to become somewhat more mellow, if a bit spacy.

Sunday, 18th

☽	#	♄	5:54
☽	☍	♄	12:58PM
☽	△	☿	6:20
☽	//	♅	7:03
☽	⚻	♀	7:09
☽	△	♂	9:07

Today's predawn, following last night's void of course, is open. Watch the very early morning for hard attitudes, but the rest of the morning should open up once again. Hard attitudes return in the early afternoon, but will pass once again. Good moods should roll in from the late afternoon through much of the evening. The energy will be mixed later. Watch for erratic relationship issues. Avoid that energy and focus instead on a fun active energy that will run through the late night. Good choices will be needed to get the most out of this day.

Monday, 19th

☽	☌	♅	1:23
☽	//	♀	8:41
☽	⚺	♆	9:16
☽	□	♃	4:28PM
☉	∠	♂	4:33
♀	□	♂	6:18
☿	△	♂	6:51
☿	⚺	♀	8:32
☽	∠	☿	11:17
☽	△	☉	11:18
☽	□	♇	11:24

There are no fewer than six major energies running through today. The first sheds light on the uses of energy and power. Much may be learned, but remember that Mars is retrograde and focus on lessons from the past. The second easily brings problems to relationships. Watch for conflict involving anything, but specifically issues from the past. The third and fourth contradict the second, and with judicious and well thought out communication, problems may be minimized and benefit may actually result. On the other hand, a day out of town might be a good idea. The fifth and sixth are also related, but contradictory. They involve communication about and light being shed on things normally kept secret and hidden. This complex of energy will probably sweep past most people, but those caught up in it will likely not soon forget it. Be aware that the Moon will be void of course from 11:24 tonight well into tomorrow's predawn.

Tuesday, 20th

☿	∠	♇	12:27
☉	⚺	♇	12:49

High energy from yesterday will remain very much with us today, and those caught up in it will remain embroiled.

☽	—	♈	3:23
☽	#	♀	8:15
☽	∠	♆	10:40
☉	∠	♀	11:11
☽	⚻	♄	4:25PM
☽	#	♅	7:56
☽	□	♂	11:35

There is another major energy today that is related to it and continues to shed light on relationship issues, but in a cautionary rather than positive way. Those not caught up in this energy should be kind and supportive to those who are. It's not going to be a pretty picture for some people. Last night's Moon void of course period ends at 3:23 this morning when the Moon enters Aries. At that point the energy will lift and general moods will tend to become more assertive and aggressive. This is not likely to be a good thing for those having problems. Watch the morning for relationship issues and spaciness. Much of the afternoon opens somewhat, but the late afternoon has hard attitudes followed by erratic irritability and mood swings in the evening, followed by aggressive attitudes in the late night. Choices.

Wednesday, 21st

☽	∠	☉	2:04
☽	☍	♀	2:11
☽	⚻	☿	3:06
☽	⚺	♅	3:49
☽	//	♄	7:57
☿	△	♅	9:57
☽	□	♆	11:15
☽	∠	♄	4:54PM
☽	△	♃	6:42
♀	⚻	♅	11:23

High energy from the past couple of days will continue strongly through today. There are three more major energies to deal with. The first is very positive for communication and transportation, especially where electricity, electronic media, and technology are involved. This energy can also be fun and innovative. Unusual approaches can work to great benefit. This may help some people during this difficult period. The second unfortunately aggravates the complex and those having trouble will not be helped by it. Watch for erratic behavior in relationships, and avoid sudden unrealistic and unreasonable demands for change. Damage control will be very important. Try to ride the storm out before making any binding decisions. Minor aspects are mixed throughout the day and good choices will definitely be in order.

Thursday, 22nd - Thanksgiving Day

☽	△	♇	12:38
☿	//	♆	3:33
☽	#	♆	3:48
☽	#	☿	3:49
☽	∠	♅	3:57
☽	⚻	☉	3:59
☽	—	♉	4:18
☉	—	♐	8:49
☽	#	♇	11:05
☽	△	♄	4:50PM
☽	∠	♃	6:53
☽	□	♂	11:15

Remember the difficult complex from the past few days as it will tend to extend through today. Be aware that the Moon will be void of course this morning from 12:38 until 4:18 when it enters Taurus. At that point the energy will lift and general moods will tend to become more down to earth and concerned with enjoyment. There are two major energies running through the day. The first is very positive for beginning projects involving prayer, meditation, and spiritual matters. Be open to the intuitive process and pay attention to guidance as it is received. The second is the Sun's entry into the mutable fire sign Sagittarius. This signals the final third of the fall harvest season. During this period, continue to reap and store the harvest from the projects be-

Pacific Time   November 2007

☽ ∠ ♇	12:25
☽ # ☉	1:18
☽ □ ⛢	3:37
☽ ⚻ ♀	5:52
☽ ☍ ☿	8:18
☽ □ ♆	10:52
☽ # ♃	3:27PM
☽ ⚻ ♃	6:46
☽ ∠ ♂	10:36

☽ ⚻ ♆	12:00
⛢ D	2:16
☽ ∥ ♂	3:07
☽ – ♊	3:29
☽ ☍ ☉	6:30
☽ ∠ ♀	7:16
☿ □ ♆	9:49
☽ □ ♄	4:03PM
☽ ⚺ ♂	9:58

☽ □ ⛢	2:44
☽ △ ♀	8:51
☽ △ ♆	10:08
☿ ∥ ♇	11:44

gun back at the vernal equinox, and begin to think about what you might want to start at the beginning of the next solar cycle. Watch the late morning to midday for potential minor coercive irritability. Moods will improve through the afternoon and a disciplined approach will serve best. Good moods should continue through the evening and into the late night. Have a good time.

Friday, 23rd

You will notice energy levels rising throughout today as tomorrow morning's full Moon comes into focus. Consider tonight and tomorrow night to be full Moon. And remember that full Moons are always high energy and deserve to be approached with respect. There may be a downturn through the early predawn, but good moods return through the mid predawn. Watch for another downturn through the morning with relationship issues, general irritability, and spaciness. Also be aware that the Moon will be void of course from 10:52 this morning through much of tomorrow's predawn. Try to have fun tonight, but remember the full Moon and the void of course.

Saturday, 24th

Yesterday's Moon void of course period runs through much of today's predawn and finally ends at 3:29 this morning when the Moon enters Gemini. At that point the energy will lift and general moods will tend to become more communicative. Today is full Moon day. It is exact at 6:30 this morning. Consider the full Moon to run through today, tomorrow, and on into Monday. There is a major energy running through today that is cautionary. Watch for major spaciness, the inebriated, and otherwise out of it. Confusion will be rampant Aside from the major energies, there may be minor relationship issues in the early morning, but this will pass quickly if it is noticed at all. Most of the rest of the daytime is open, but watch the late afternoon to early evening for a period of potential hard attitudes. Once past that, moods will improve and should remain positive through the late night. This will be a more positive, social evening than last night was.

Sunday, 25th

Remember to consider the full Moon as very active through today. There are two more major energies. The first is very good for looking within and coming to deeper self understanding. That which is normally kept secret and hidden

Astro-Weather   137

☽	⚻	☿	12:55PM
☽	☍	♃	6:51
☽	☍	♇	11:38

will be more accessible than usual. The second, on higher octaves, is very good for taking relationships to more spiritual places. This energy may also be used socially, however, and that is how most will approach it. There may be some minor erratic irritability in the mid predawn, but this will likely pass unnoticed. Good moods will run through the morning. Make good use. The early afternoon may have a brief period of erratic irritability, but this again should be easily dealt with. Watch for exaggerated emotional reactions in the early evening, but moods should be predominantly positive. Be aware that the Moon will be void of course from 11:38 tonight into tomorrow's predawn.

Monday, 26th

♀	△	♆	1:54
☽	—	♋	3:07
☽	⚻	☉	9:46
☽	∠	♆	10:21
☽	∠	☿	4:04PM
☽	□	♄	4:20
☽	☌	♂	9:54

Last night's Moon void of course period ends at 3:07 this morning when the Moon enters Cancer. At that point the energy will lift and general moods will tend to become more sensitive and protective. The rest of the predawn though early morning following the void of course will be open. Watch the rest of the morning, however, for irritability and spaciness. Most of the afternoon opens up, but the late afternoon is mixed. Take a friendly yet disciplined approach and avoid any tendency toward argumentativeness. The evening opens up and an active approach is indicated for the late night.

Tuesday, 27th

☽	△	♅	3:26
☽	⚻	♆	11:19
☽	∠	☉	12:36PM
☽	//	♂	12:39
☽	□	♀	2:12
☽	∠	♄	5:34
☽	△	☿	8:24
☽	⚻	♃	9:21

There will be a major energy that peaks tomorrow morning coming into focus throughout today. This is high positive energy for any project or activity involving communication and transportation. Make good use of this as it will be possible to get a lot done. Most of today's predawn is open. Good moods will run through the mid predawn and an innovative approach will work best. Most of the morning is open, but watch the late morning to the early evening for spaciness, irritability, relationship issues, and hard attitudes coming up in that order. Moods will improve through the evening, but be aware that the Moon will be void of course from 8:24 tonight through most of tomorrow's predawn.

Wednesday, 28th

☽	⚻	♇	1:47
☽	#	♃	2:55
☽	∠	♅	5:01
☽	—	♌	5:24
☿	⚺	♃	6:11

Last night's Moon void of course period will run through the predawn and end at 5:24 this morning when the Moon enters Leo. At that point the energy will lift and general moods will tend to become more intense and concerned with self. The high positive energy mentioned yesterday

Pacific Time   November 2007

♀ ∥ ♅	12:58PM
☽ # ☉	1:18
☽ △ ☉	4:36
☿ ∠ ♂	4:52
☽ ⚻ ♄	7:48

will remain very much with us through today. It is joined by two more major energies. The first is positive for artistic endeavors and taking relationships to more unusual places. Plan some sort of fun and stimulating activity and be open to innovative social scenes. The second can be more problematic for communication and transportation, especially where aggressive attitudes are indulged and force is threatened or used. Go for it through the workday. Good moods will be dominant especially from the late afternoon through the evening and into the late night.

Thursday, 29th

☽ ∠ ♃	12:05
☽ ⚻ ♂	12:55
☽ # ☿	2:24
☽ ∠ ♆	4:19
☽ ⚺ ♅	7:39
♀ ∠ ♄	8:46
☽ # ♇	11:03
☽ ☍ ♆	4:12PM
☽ # ♆	7:35
☿ ⚻ ♇	9:24

High energy from yesterday, both positive and otherwise, will tend to linger through today. Reread and apply. There are two more major energies running through today. The first can bring problems to relationships, especially where hard, cold attitudes are indulged. If trouble pops up, switch to damage control and ride it out. Anyone seriously falling prey to this energy will find consequences harsher and longer lasting than usual. The second is very good for looking beneath the surface and coming to deeper understanding. Things normally kept secret and hidden will be more accessible than usual, but in a more positive way. There is scattered minor irritability throughout the day and good choices will be needed to deal with it successfully.

Friday, 30th

☽ □ ♀	12:27
☽ ∠ ♂	3:54
☽ △ ♃	3:57
☽ △ ♆	7:59
☽ □ ☿	9:26
☽ — ♍	11:45
☉ □ ♄	12:22PM
☽ ∥ ♄	7:02

High energy from the past couple of days should be taken into account through today as well. There is another major energy that is definitely of the cautionary persuasion. Be serious about self discipline issues. Watch for people running into all manner of restriction and frustration and avoid any acting out on it. This energy also easily brings about problems with and for authority and this is definitely not the day to smart off to the boss. Aside from the major energies, good moods should be dominant through the predawn and early morning. Watch the mid morning for a brief period of argumentativeness and be aware that the Moon will be void of course this morning from 9:26 until 11:45 when it enters Virgo. At that point the energy will lift and general moods will tend to become more discerning and concerned with detail. Have fun tonight, but remember the cautionary energy and be careful.

Astro-Weather

December 2007

Overview

As December opens, Jupiter will be moving away from last month's sextile to Neptune and toward a conjunction with Pluto. It will peak on the 11th and will be very strong throughout the month. This is a very positive aspect for deep changes on all levels. There should have been gains in the peace movement last month that will increase this month. It remains vital that we all participate in any prayer and meditation for peace efforts as get organized.

On more personal levels, Mars will be retrograde throughout the month. This will tend to energize those mired in conflict from the international level all the way down to individual disputes. Be especially wary wherever old altercations have potential to reignite. We have a highly cautionary day on the 6th into the 7th to be prepared for. Be especially careful around the new Moon as the full Moon has exceedingly high attendant energy. Be very careful in any situation involving old and long standing disputes. The 20th is a day for making many kinds of new beginnings. There are many other major energy days to read ahead and make plans for dealing with. The most significant daytime Moon void of course periods are on the 7th, 12th, 21st and the 25th. There are a few half day voids to work around as well.

Saturday, 1st

☽ ☌ ♄	3:27
☽ # ♀	4:13
☿ – ♐	4:20
☽ ☐ ☉	4:44
☽ ⚹ ♀	7:41
☽ ⚹ ♂	7:52
☽ # ♅	8:39
☽ ☍ ♅	4:04PM

The high cautionary energy mentioned yesterday will remain with us through today. Reread and apply, being especially careful in any encounter with authority. There are two more major energies today. The first indicates a general shift in thinking and communication patterns toward a more expansive and open mode. The second is high social energy, pure and simple. Party people will be in their glory. Have fun with them or get out of their way. The late predawn has a period of potentially very bad moods. The lucky will sleep through it. The early morning is mixed. Take an active, friendly approach and watch for relationship issues and erratic emotional responses. Most of the rest of the daytime is open, but watch the late afternoon to early evening for another brief period of erratic emotional responses. Make good choices and have a great time through the rest of the evening and late night.

Pacific Time   December 2007

♀	⚹	♃	12:14
☽	⊼	♆	1:19
☉	⊼	♂	12:26PM
☽	□	♃	2:51
☽	⚻	♀	4:05
☽	□	♇	6:12
☽	−	♎	10:01

Sunday, 2ⁿᵈ
The high social energy mentioned yesterday will remain very much with us through today. Have fun with it. There is another major energy, however, that is decidedly more cautionary. Watch for all manner of erratic behavior up to and including violence. This may or may not involve authority figures. Light may be shed on the uses of energy and power, but in an erratic and potentially troubling manner. All of this is likely to involve issues from the past. Minor aspects are mixed and good choices will be needed. Be aware that the Moon will be void of course tonight from 6:12 until 10:01 when it enters Libra. At that point the energy will lift and general moods will tend to become more concerned with balance and beauty.

☽	⚹	☿	4:15
☽	□	♆	7:06
♀	⚹	♇	2:34PM
☽	⚻	♄	2:42
☽	∥	♅	5:28
☽	□	♂	5:57
☽	⚹	☉	9:24

Monday, 3ʳᵈ
Continue to observe yesterday's cautions through today. There is another major energy that can be positive for taking relationships to deeper levels. There is a strong sexual component to this energy, however, and it needs to be handled carefully. Most of today's predawn is open. Take a friendly and communicative approach through the late predawn. There may be a brief period of minor spaciness in the early morning, but this is likely to pass quickly if it is noticed at all. The rest of the morning through much of the afternoon is open. Take a disciplined approach through the mid afternoon and get a lot done. Watch for aggressive attitudes in the early evening but good moods will dominate the late night.

☽	∥	♀	3:26
☽	⊼	♅	3:45
☽	#	♄	7:48
☽	△	♆	1:22PM
☽	∠	☿	3:02
☽	∠	♄	9:04

Tuesday, 4ᵗʰ
There is a major energy coming into focus throughout the day that can bring problems to relationships. Watch for erratic and bizarre behavior and beware of unreasonable and unrealistic demands for change. Some will attempt to use this energy socially, which is not impossible, but does require careful attention. Watch the mid predawn to early morning for minor erratic emotional reactions. The early morning may have a short burst of hard attitudes. The early through mid afternoon is mixed. Take a friendly approach, be open to the intuitive process, but watch for minor irritability and argumentativeness. The later evening may have another short period of hard attitudes. Choices.

♀	⚻	♅	1:53

Wednesday, 5ᵗʰ
Yesterday's tricky energy involving relationships and social

Astro-Weather

☽	⚹	♃	4:21
♀	→	♏	5:28
☽	∠	☉	6:35
☽	⚹	♇	6:48
☽	//	♆	9:18
☽	⚼	♅	10:09
☽	→	♏	10:30
☽	☌	♀	11:03
☽	//	♇	7:03PM

activities will remain with us through today. Reread. There is another major energy that indicates a general shift in relationships and aesthetics toward a deeper and more intense mode. Aside from the major energies, most of today's predawn is open. The late predawn through early morning is mixed. Take an expansive, friendly and cooperative approach, avoiding any minor irritabilities that may pop up. Be aware that the Moon will be void of course this morning from 6:48 until 10:30 when it enters Scorpio. At that point the energy will lift noticeably and general moods will tend to become more intense. Pay attention to relationships following the void of course. The afternoon into the evening is open. Take a cooperative approach through the later evening and into the late night.

Thursday, 6th

☽	⚺	☿	2:06
☽	⚹	♄	3:34
☽	△	♂	5:18
☽	∠	♃	11:22
♀	#	♄	12:54PM
☿	□	♄	1:16
☽	∠	♇	1:18
☽	⚺	☉	3:51
☽	△	♅	4:36
☿	⚻	♂	10:58

There are four major energies running through the day, all of which are of a cautionary nature. The first easily brings problems to relationships, especially where feelings of restriction and frustration are indulged and acted out on. The second is much like the first except that it involves communication and transportation. Many people will run into limitations and restrictions that they will not respond to favorably. The third stimulates erratic behavior that easily ignites conflicts of all kinds. Be very careful in traffic and watch for old disputes to reappear. The fourth would be plenty cautionary all on its own and is in very bad combination with the other three. Watch for erratic and bizarre behavior of all kinds as it will be crazies on parade throughout the day. Be very careful in any dealings with authority, which can turn on you in an instant. Aside from the major energies, minor aspects tend to be positive. Good moods are not out of the question, just watch for those in the throes of the cautionary energies.

Friday, 7th

☉	□	♅	12:34
☽	//	☿	1:05
☽	□	♆	2:16
☽	//	☉	3:57
☽	//	♃	8:33
☽	⚼	♂	10:54
☽	⚺	♃	6:15PM
☽	⚺	♇	7:41
☽	→	♐	11:10

High energy from yesterday will remain very much with us through today. Reread and apply the cautions carefully. Take a communicative approach through today's early predawn. Watch the early predawn for spaciness. Do be aware that the Moon will be void of course today from 2:16 this morning until 11:10 tonight when the Moon enters Sagittarius. At that point the energy will lift very noticeably and general moods will tend to become more expansive and open to a wide range of ideas. Try to relax and take it easy through the void of course and tend to old business. There

☽ ⊻ ♀	6:18	
☽ # ♂	8:09	
☽ □ ♄	4:08PM	
☽ ⊼ ♂	4:14	
♂ ✶ ♄	7:58	
☉ ∥ ☿	10:20	
☽ ☌ ☿	11:39	

☽ □ ♅	4:55	
☽ ☌ ☉	9:39	
☽ ✶ ♆	2:27PM	
☽ ∠ ♀	3:27	

☽ ☌ ♃	7:08	
☽ ☌ ♇	7:35	
☿ ∥ ♃	9:42	
☽ — ♑	10:50	
☿ □ ♅	4:24PM	
☽ ∠ ♆	8:03	

may be some minor aggressive irritability in the late morning, but this will pass quickly. Moods should lighten through the evening. Have fun tonight, but be mindful of the lingering cautionary energies and the void of course, and don't take new things too seriously.

Saturday, 8th

There are three major energies today. The first would normally be positive for any project involving the uses of energy and power. This may still be the case, but remember that Mars is retrograde. Use this energy to complete projects from the past. The second is positive for looking within, coming to greater self understanding, and initiating positive change. You will notice energy levels rising throughout the day as the third major energy, tomorrow's new Moon, rolls in. Have fun tonight but remember the new Moon and be good.

Sunday, 9th

Today is new Moon day. It is exact at 9:39 this morning. Remember that what you start at new Moon brings results at the next full Moon. It always pays to start things that you would like to see the results of. This particular new to full period is very high energy and should be handled carefully. Be mindful of any potential disputes, especially from the past. Aside from the major energy, watch the late predawn for erratic emotional responses. Most of the daytime is open. Take a friendly approach through the mid to late afternoon and watch for relationship issues.

Monday, 10th

Consider the new Moon to run through today and well into tomorrow at least. There are two more major energies today. They are related and contradictory. The first is very good for beginning any sort of project involving communication and transportation. The second easily brings problems to the same areas, especially where electricity, electronic media and technology are involved. This energy also brings out the nutballs. Watch for erratic and bizarre behavior of all kinds. The Moon will be void of course this morning from 7:35 until 10:50 this afternoon when it enters Capricorn. At that point the energy will lift noticeably and general moods will tend to become more down to earth and concerned with accomplishment. The afternoon through the evening following the void of course is open. Watch for minor spaciness later.

☽	⚹	♀	12:07
☽	☍	♂	1:57
☽	△	♄	3:30
♃	☌	♇	11:35
♀	△	♂	3:15PM
☽	⚹	♅	3:57
☽	#	♂	4:20
☽	⚺	☿	7:19
☉	⚹	♆	7:47

Tuesday, 11th

There are three major energies running throughout the day. The first is a long range outer planet aspect that may well stimulate some interesting headlines. This should most likely involve good news about things beneath the surface and normally kept hidden. Watch the news. The second is very positive for relationships, especially the male-female variety. Make a positive gesture in an appropriate situation and it may be reciprocated. The third is very positive for any prayer, meditation, or spiritual practice one may be involved in. This energy can also be taken socially, which is what many will do with it. Moods should be more positive than otherwise throughout the day, but get anything important done before 3:57 this afternoon as the Moon will be void of course from then through most of tomorrow.

☽	⚺	♆	1:17
☽	⚺	☉	1:45
☽	⚼	♄	8:35
♀	⚹	♄	11:32
☽	//	☿	12:43PM
☽	//	♃	4:49
☽	//	☉	5:38
☽	⚺	♇	6:02
☽	⚺	♃	6:30
☽	∠	♅	8:51
☽	–	♒	9:00

Wednesday, 12th

Yesterday's Moon void of course period runs through most of today and finally ends at 9:00 tonight when the Moon enters Aquarius. At that point the energy will lift very noticeably and general moods will tend to become more independent and free thinking. Relax and take it easy through the void of course, tending to old business. There is a major energy running throughout the day that is very positive for strengthening and solidifying relationships. Make good use of this but remember the void of course and don't take new things too seriously. Moods should be more positive than otherwise throughout the day and evening.

☽	∠	☿	4:16
☽	∠	☉	9:00
☽	⚻	♂	10:07
☽	⚻	♄	1:14PM
☽	□	♀	3:51
☿	⚹	♆	7:01
☽	∠	♇	10:33
☽	∠	♃	11:27

Thursday, 13th

There is a major energy running throughout today that is very positive for any prayer, meditation, or spiritual practice one may be involved in. This energy can also be taken socially, which is what many will do with it. Aside from the major energy, most of the predawn is open, but watch the late predawn for a brief period of minor irritability. Most of the morning is open, but the mid through late morning has more of the same along with an erratic aggressiveness. Watch the early through mid afternoon for hard attitudes and relationship issues. Things should lighten up through the evening.

☽	⚺	♅	1:18
☽	//	♇	3:44
☽	☌	♆	10:20

Friday, 14th

Positive energy mentioned yesterday will remain with us today. Reread. Those involved in these kinds of things should make good use of it. There is another major energy coming

☽	⚹	☿	12:26PM
☽	∥	♆	12:58
☽	⚼	♂	1:29
☽	⚹	☉	3:35
☉	∥	♃	7:32
☽	∥	♀	10:19

into focus throughout the day. This is high positive energy, pure and simple. Many will be feeling confident, good about themselves, and have a general sense of wellbeing. The only problem with this energy is the tendency to get carried away and overindulge. The predawn may start out with minor irritability and erratic emotional reactions, but this will pass quickly and good moods follow. Be open to the intuitive process through the morning and midday. The afternoon is mixed, but with the right choices, good moods will prevail. This will be a high energy social Friday night.

Saturday, 15th

☽	⚹	♇	2:32
☽	⚹	♃	3:50
☽	→	♓	5:14
☽	#	♄	11:53
☽	△	♂	4:18PM
☽	☍	♄	8:49

High positive energy from yesterday will remain with us through today. Use it well. Late Friday night social scenes are likely to be energized well into today's predawn. Good moods should run through the predawn, but be aware that the Moon will be void of course this morning from 3:50 until 5:14 when it enters Pisces. At that point the energy will lift and general moods will tend to become somewhat more mellow, if a bit spacy. The morning following the void of course is open. Watch the midday for a brief period of hard attitudes. Good moods should return in the late afternoon to early evening. There may be a return of hard attitudes and cold emotional reactions into the later evening. Have fun tonight, but choose well.

Sunday, 16th

☽	∥	♅	12:53
☽	△	♀	4:42
☽	☌	♅	8:22
☽	⚺	♆	5:01PM
♀	∠	♇	5:58

There is a major energy running throughout today that easily leads to a heavy and potentially coercive sexuality. As always with this energy, protect the vulnerable. Be open to innovation through the early predawn. The late predawn has good moods. The earlier, innovative energy runs through the early to mid morning. Most of the afternoon is open and good moods should return in the late afternoon to early evening. Have fun today and tonight, but remember the caution.

Monday, 17th

☽	□	☿	2:02
☽	□	☉	2:16
☉	☌	☿	7:26
☽	□	♇	8:26
☽	⚼	♀	9:45
☽	□	♃	10:25
☽	→	♈	10:51
♀	∠	♃	7:07PM

The high cautionary energy mentioned yesterday will continue through today. It is joined by three more major energies. The first is very good for introspection and coming to greater self-understanding. The second and third are related and are intensely social. This is energy better suited to a weekend and this being a Monday ... Problems with this energy occur through getting carried away and falling into overindulgence. On the other hand, you may want to plan

December 2007   Pacific Time

☽	∠	♆	7:17
☽	□	♂	7:54
♀	△	♅	10:43

some sort of unusual, stimulating, and fun activity with those closest to you. Aside from the major energies, there is scattered irritability from the mid predawn through the morning. Watch the mid predawn for a period of intensely bad moods. There is a short Moon void of course period this morning from 10:25 until 10:51 when the Moon enters Aries. At that point the energy will lift and general moods will tend to become more assertive and aggressive. Good choices can yield a fun day, but it will be easy to let the little things spoil it.

Tuesday, 18th

☽	⚻	♄	1:38
☽	#	♅	2:46
♃	→	♑	12:11PM
☽	⚼	♅	12:37
☽	⚻	♀	1:52
☽	∥	♄	3:03
♂	⚇	♆	5:10
☽	✶	♆	8:48

High energy from yesterday will tend to linger through today. Reread and make good use of it. There are two more major energies running through the day. The first is a general shift in religious and philosophical energy toward a more down to earth and disciplined mode. The second is cautionary. Watch for spacy, unfocused violence and be very careful around water and hot or caustic liquids and gases. This is an explosive energy that can flare up unexpectedly. Do not let minor disputes escalate. Minor aspects are of little help through the day and good choices are highly recommended. Things should lighten up and better moods roll in through the late night.

Wednesday, 19th

☽	⚇	♄	2:58
♄	℞		6:10
☽	△	☉	9:21
☽	#	♀	9:56
☿	☌	♇	10:50
☽	△	♇	11:27
☽	△	☿	11:31
☽	#	♆	11:47
☽	→	♉	1:37PM
☽	∠	♅	1:42
☽	△	♃	2:01
☽	#	♇	8:17
☽	✶	♂	8:54

The high cautionary energy mentioned yesterday will tend to remain with us through today. Reread and apply carefully. There is another major energy today that provides access to information and things normally kept secret and hidden. Keep your eyes and ears open as there is likely to be much to learn. This energy is also very good for initiating positive changes on deep levels. Understanding is the key. Aside from the major energies, today's early predawn is open. Watch the mid predawn for a brief period of hard attitudes. Good moods should run from the mid morning into the midday, but watch for some potential relationship issues. Be aware that the Moon will be void of course today from 11:31 this morning until 1:37 this afternoon when it enters Taurus. At that point the energy will lift and general moods will tend to become more down to earth and concerned with enjoyment. The afternoon following the void of course is mixed. Take a friendly and expansive approach, avoiding erratic emotional responses. The evening is open, but the late night is mixed again. Take an active, fun approach, but watch for some potential coercive irritability.

☽	△	♄	3:40
☿	→	♑	6:42
☽	⚼	☉	11:44
☽	⚼	♇	12:03PM
☿	☌	♃	1:53
☽	⚹	♅	2:13
☽	⚼	♃	2:53
☽	⚼	☿	3:00
☉	☌	♇	4:17
♀	//	♆	4:58
☽	☍	♀	7:40
☽	∠	♂	8:38
☽	□	♆	10:05

Thursday, 20th

There are five major energies running through the day. The first indicates a general shift in thinking and communication patterns toward a more down to earth and concerned with accomplishment mode. The second is very positive for beginning any project involving communication and transportation. The third sheds light on things normally kept secret and hidden, but in a more positive way than often occurs. This energy is very good for beginning any sort of self transformation at very deep levels. Keep an eye on authority figures in your life as there may be much to learn in those areas. The fourth can be used socially, which is how many will approach it, but on higher octaves it is excellent for dealing with relationships and aesthetics on more spiritual levels. The fifth, which peaks early tomorrow morning, can bring problems to relationships. Choose to get along and seek not to impose your will on others, and be especially careful not to fall into old problems. Minor aspects are mixed at best. Make good choices and use the positive energies well. Do be aware that the Moon will be void of course from 10:05 tonight through much of tomorrow.

☽	#	♃	2:21
☽	#	☉	3:23
♀	⚼	♂	4:58
☽	⚻	♇	12:15PM
☽	⚻	☉	1:39
☽	→	♊	2:14
☽	#	☿	2:30
☽	⚻	♃	3:23
☽	⚻	☿	5:57
☽	⚺	♂	8:05
☉	→	♑	10:07

Friday, 21st

Last night's Moon void of course period runs through most of the day and finally ends at 2:14 this afternoon when the Moon enters Gemini. At that point the energy will lift very noticeably and general moods will tend to become more communicative. The cautionary relationship energy mentioned yesterday will remain with us through today and should be handled carefully. There are two more major energies. The first is the Sun's entry into the cardinal earth sign Capricorn. This is the Winter Solstice and the beginning of the first third of the winter season. During this time you will want to plan for your major projects to be started at the vernal equinox in March. The second is more cautionary relationship energy. Watch for spaciness and confusion, especially where recreational substances have been overindulged and the otherwise out of it are involved. Damage control. This will be a high energy social Friday night, but one to be very careful with.

♀	□	♆	2:21
☽	□	♄	3:55
☽	//	♂	4:03
☿	☍	♂	10:28

Saturday, 22nd

High energy from yesterday will remain very much with us through today, especially the spacy relationship variety. There are three more major energies running through today. The first can bring problems to communication and trans-

☽	□	♅	2:24PM
☉	☌	♃	9:55
☽	△	♆	10:13
☽	⚻	♀	11:54

portation, especially where people become pushy and aggressive. Be careful in traffic. Remember that Mars is retrograde and be on the lookout for issues and disputes from the past to recur. The second is high positive energy itself, which can be used for anything. Initiate positive changes of all kinds. You will notice energy levels rising throughout the day as the third major energy, tomorrow's full Moon, rolls in. This will be a very high energy social Saturday night. Make wise choices.

Sunday, 23rd

☿	∠	♆	10:25
☽	☍	♇	12:26PM
☽	→	♋	2:18
☽	☍	♃	4:12
☽	☍	☉	5:15
☽	☌	♂	6:59
☽	⚼	♆	10:27
☽	☍	☿	11:53

Today is full Moon day. It is exact at 5:15 this afternoon. Remember that full Moons are always high energy and deserve to be approached with respect. This is a very high energy full Moon that can go either way. There is very positive energy for change, but there is also the potential for flare-ups of old disputes. Choices will be very important. Late Saturday night social scenes will be very highly energized. Have fun but be careful. Minor aspects are of very little help through the day and choices will be very important. Be aware of a Moon void of course period this afternoon from 12:26 until 2:18 when the Moon enters Cancer. At that point the energy will lift noticeably and general moods will tend to become more sensitive and protective.

Monday, 24th

☽	⚼	♀	2:16
☽	⚹	♄	4:10
☽	//	♂	7:39
☉	☍	♂	11:46
☽	△	♅	3:03PM
☽	#	☿	10:45
☽	⚻	♆	11:10

Consider the full Moon and attendant energies, both positive and cautionary, to run through today and tomorrow. There is another major energy that will turn this into a very high energy day that can go either way. Light will be shed on the uses of energy and power. Problems and disputes from the past will receive similar illumination. Forgive and let go. The alternative would be poorly timed, to say the least. Family gatherings today and tomorrow can be very positive or very not. Choose very wisely. Aside from the major energies, the predawn through early morning is mixed. With a friendly and disciplined approach, good moods will be available. Most of the daytime is open. Good moods will run through the mid afternoon. Make the right choices to keep the glow going.

Tuesday, 25th – Christmas Day

☽	∠	♄	4:57
☽	△	♀	5:17
☽	#	☉	10:42
☽	#	♃	11:35

High energy from yesterday will remain with us through today. Choices will be of the utmost importance. There is a major energy running through the day that is very positive. This energy is excellent for communication, transportation,

☽	⚻	♇	2:02PM
☿	△	♄	3:09
☽	→	♌	3:52
☽	⚼	♅	4:12
☽	⚻	♃	6:43
☽	⚺	♂	7:27
☽	⚻	☉	10:53

discussion, and coming to long term agreement. This is the disciplined communication energy to focus on and stay with. The late predawn through early morning is mixed. Avoid hard attitudes and choose rather fun and enjoyment. The Moon will be void of course today from 5:17 this morning until 3:52 this afternoon when it enters Leo. At that point the energy will lift very noticeably and general moods will tend to become more intense and focused on self. Relax, take it easy, and have fun through the void. Do be prepared for a huge rush of energy as it ends. Minor aspects are mixed throughout the day and into the late night. Make the best possible choices.

Wednesday, 26th

☽	⚺	♄	6:30
☽	⚻	☿	8:32
♂	☍	♃	11:52
☽	⚼	♇	3:58PM
☽	⚻	♅	6:13
☽	#	♇	7:29
☽	#	♀	7:47
☽	∠	♂	8:48
☽	⚼	♃	9:13
☉	∠	♆	10:40

High energy continues through today with the addition of three more major energies. The first signifies an excess of energy itself. Normally this would be more positive, but Mars remains retrograde and any disputes from the past that reignite will have a tendency to blow up all out of proportion. Go ahead and try to use the energy positively, but be prepared to back off at a moment's notice. The second brings out the space cases. Watch for spaciness and confusion of all kinds, especially where intoxicants have been overindulged and the otherwise out of it are involved. These first two energies can be a bad combination. The third is good for taking relationships to deeper levels and initiating positive change. There may be a sexual component to this that will need to be handled carefully. Minor aspects are of little to no help through today and choices remain important.

Thursday, 27th

♀	//	♇	1:05
☽	☍	♆	2:53
☽	⚼	☉	3:13
☽	#	♆	4:59
☿	∠	♀	8:34
☽	□	♀	2:33PM
☽	⚼	☿	2:45
☽	△	♇	6:54
☽	→	♍	8:45
☽	⚹	♂	11:04

The high cautionary energy mentioned yesterday will remain with us through today. Reread and apply the warnings. The relationship energy from yesterday will stay with us as well. There is another major energy to deal with today that can bring some problems to relationships. Watch for a general disagreeableness and don't let minor annoyances build up into real confrontations. Aside from the major energies, watch the mid through late predawn for spaciness and irritability. The morning through most of the afternoon is open. There may be some minor relationship issues and argumentativeness in the mid to late afternoon, but good moods will roll in through the evening. Be aware that the Moon will be void of course tonight from 6:54 until 8:45 when it enters Virgo. At that point the energy will lift and general moods

December 2007   Pacific Time

will become more discerning and concerned with detail.

Friday, 28th

☽	△	♃	12:45
☽	∥	♄	2:48
☽	△	☉	8:52
☽	☌	♄	12:26PM
☽	#	♅	4:57
☽	△	☿	10:32
☉	∥	♃	11:21

There will be an energy coming into focus throughout the day that is very positive for anything one may be involved with. The only problem with this energy is a tendency to get carried away and overindulge. Good moods should be dominant throughout the day, especially in the early predawn, morning and late night. Take a disciplined approach through the workday and get a lot done. There may be some minor irritability in the early evening, but this will pass quickly if it's noticed at all. This will be a high energy social Friday night. Have fun.

Saturday, 29th

☽	☍	♅	1:15
☽	⚻	♆	10:37
♀	⚺	♇	3:27PM
☿	✶	♅	8:10

High positive energy from yesterday will remain with us through today. Make good use of it. There are three more major energies coming into focus throughout the day. The first is very good for communication in and taking relationships to deeper levels. There may be a strong sexual component to this, however, that may need to be handled carefully. The second is great for communication and transportation, especially where electricity, electronic media and technology are involved. The third is excellent for things involving self-discipline, authority, older people and traditional matters. This a go-for-it day and a high energy social Saturday night.

Sunday, 30th

☽	□	♆	3:49
☽	✶	♀	5:08
☉	△	♄	5:23
☽	–	♎	5:37
☽	□	♂	6:24
♀	–	♐	10:01
☽	□	♃	11:00
♀	⚻	♂	3:08PM
☽	⚼	♆	3:53
☽	⚺	♄	10:16
☽	∥	♅	10:51
☽	□	☉	11:51

High positive energy from yesterday will tend to remain with us through today. Make good use of it, especially the third one mentioned as it peaks early this morning. There are two more major energies today. The first indicates a general shift in relationships and aesthetics toward a more expansive and wide ranging mode. The second, unfortunately, can bring problems to relationships. Watch for erratic behavior and sudden, unreasonable demands for change. If trouble pops up, switch to damage control and ride the storm out. There will be a short Moon void of course period this morning from 5:08 until 5:37 when the Moon enters Libra. At that point the energy will lift and general moods will tend to become more concerned with balance and beauty. There is scattered minor irritability through the day and a period of very bad moods rolling in through the very late night. Choices.

Pacific Time   December 2007

Monday, 31ˢᵗ

♂	–	♊	8:00
☽	⊼	♅	12:03PM
☽	∠	♀	2:10
☽	#	♄	2:18
☽	□	☿	6:11
☽	△	♆	9:53

Continue to observe the cautionary relationship energy mentioned yesterday through today as well. There is another major energy that indicates a general shift in the way energy and power are thought about and used toward a more communicative mode. This is Mars retrograding back into Gemini. Watch for old arguments to recur and don't take the bait when it is dangled in front of you. The early predawn has a period of intensely bad moods. The rest of the predawn through the morning is open. There is scattered irritability, relationship issues, hard attitudes and argumentativeness from the midday through the evening. Moods will improve through the late night. Make good choices and have fun tonight.

Astro-Weather

A Brief Explanation of the Aspects

Alongside the written paragraph for each day is the list of aspects and the times that they occur. They are included for those who can read them, for students who may benefit from them and to stimulate curiosity in people who may want to learn more about astrology. Most of these will consist of the symbols for the two planets that are involved, with the aspect (angle) symbol in the middle. Some will have the symbol of a planet and an arrow pointing into the symbol for one of the signs. This indicates the ingress, or entry, of the planet into that sign. Fewer will have the symbol of a planet followed by ℞ which indicates the planet turning retrograde or a D indicating that a retrograde planet is returning to direct motion.

Major Aspects

Conjunction: ☌ 0° When two or more planets occupy the same degree in a sign. Conjunctions are neutral and are aspects of beginnings. New Moons are conjunctions and are the beginning of the monthly lunar cycle.

Solar Eclipse: ☌ This is when the new Moon is lined up so that the Moon is between the Earth and the Sun and casts a shadow on parts of the Earth. It is still a conjunction of the Moon and Sun but is more intense than usual.

Semisextile: ⚺ 30° When two planets are 30 degrees apart. This is a moderately positive aspect in which the two planets are in good communication. Not considered a classical major aspect for void of course termination.

Sextile: ✶ 60° When two planets are 60 degrees apart. This is a positive aspect in which the two planets are in a harmonious relationship.

Square: □ 90° When two planets are 90 degrees apart. This is a cautionary aspect which represents an excess of the combined energy of the two planets. With the right choices this energy may be put to good use. Most often people fail to do that so the aspect has come to be viewed as difficult.

Trine: △ 120° When two planets are 120 degrees apart. This is considered to be the most positive of aspects and represents an abundance of the combined energy of the two planets.

Quincunx: ⚻ 150° When two planets are 150 degrees apart. This aspect is more cautionary than positive but is eccentric and can go either way. Its unpredictability has caused it to be viewed as difficult, but it can at times be a positive surprise. Not considered a classical major aspect for void of course termination.

Opposition: ☍ 180° When two planets are 180 degrees apart. Oppositions are aspects of manifestation. They are the opposite and culmination of conjunctions. Oppositions bring about a manifestation of the combination of the energies of the planets involved. This is a rather heavy aspect that has come to be viewed as cautionary. Full Moons, for example, are oppositions.

Lunar Eclipse: ☍ This is when the full Moon is lined up so that the Earth is between the Moon and the Sun and casts a shadow on the Moon. It is still an opposition of the Moon and Sun but is more intense than usual.

Minor Aspects

Semisquare: ∠ 45° When two planets are 45 degrees apart. This is a minor aspect that is mildly cautionary being, just as the degrees imply, half of a square.

Sesquiquadrate: ⚼ 135° When two planets are 135 degrees apart. This is a minor aspect that is mildly irritable but quite often passes unnoticed.

Parallel: ∥ When two planets are in the same degree of declination north or south of the equator. This aspect is to be viewed as being much the same as a conjunction.

Contraparallel: ⌗ When two planets are in the same degree north and south of the equator. This aspect is to be viewed as being much the same as an opposition.

Ingress → When a planet leaves one sign and enters another.

The Planets and Signs

The Planets

Much more can be said of the planets and signs than is explained here. The following is a brief glance at the essence of each of them as it relates specifically to Astro-Weather.

Sun: ☉ Light, Illumination, Authority.

Moon: ☽ Emotion, Mood, Feeling.

Mercury: ☿ Communication and transportation. The thinking and communication process. Travel, Traffic, Commerce.

Venus: ♀ Relationships, the Arts.

Mars: ♂ Energy, Power, Action.

Jupiter: ♃ General Positivity, Expansiveness, Preservation.

Saturn: ♄ Discipline, Limitation. Imposition of authority. Older people. Tradition.

Uranus: ♅ Eccentricity, Craziness, the Unusual. Electricity, Technology, Magic.

Neptune: ♆ Spaciness, Inebriants, Spirituality.

Pluto: ♇ All things secret and hidden. Sexuality, Coerciveness.

The Signs

More often than not, when you see the signs listed it is when the Moon is entering a sign at the end of a Moon void of course period. Again, what you will find below is the essence of the sign as it relates to Astro-Weather and is by no means meant to be seen as a complete explanation. Think of these as keywords.

Aries: ♈ Assertive and aggressive.

Taurus: ♉ Down to earth and concerned with enjoyment.

Gemini: ♊ Communicative.

Cancer: ♋ Sensitive and protective.

Leo: ♌ Intense and concerned with self.

Virgo: ♍ Critical, discerning and concerned with detail.

Libra: ♎ Concerned with balance, beauty and harmony.

Scorpio: ♏ Intense, secretive, deep.

Sagittarius: ♐ Widely and deeply free-ranging. Open to a wide range of ideas.

Capricorn: ♑ Disciplined, down to earth and concerned with accomplishment.

Aquarius: ♒ Innovative, independent, free-thinking.

Pisces: ♓ Intuitive, spaciness, concern for and appreciation of intangibles.

Lightworks.com & The Monthly Aspectarian

Lightworks.com, the publisher of *Astro-Weather Reports,* is also the publisher of *The Monthly Aspectarian* magazine, available locally in the greater Chicago area and nationally by subscription.

Published since 1979, *The Monthly Aspectarian* magazine has been "Dedicated to Awakening Consciousness," focusing our efforts in the areas of personal growth, healthy and holistic living, spiritual transformation, and global awareness. Today *The Monthly Aspectarian* is regarded as the foremost voice in the greater Chicago area for those seeking to enhance body, mind, and spirit. Here you will find outstanding feature articles by nationally known writers, regular monthly columns on topics of interest, interviews with best-selling authors and personalities, special editorial sections, plus current happenings, reviews, and directories of products, services, and events.

Guy Spiro's Original
Astro-Weather Report
Published Continuously Since 1979

The *Astro-Weather Report* is published annually in four editions, one for each of the four time zones of the continental United States. Readers may place their orders in advance for the next edition which will be shipped as soon as it becomes available.

ORDER FORM

2008 Astro-Weather Report ($16.95 each)	Qty.	Amt.
Eastern Time Zone Edition		
Central Time Zone Edition		
Mountain Time Zone Edition		
Pacific Time Zone Edition		
Subtotal		
Illinois residents add 8.75% tax ($1.48 per book)		
Shipping & handling ($3.50 per book)		
TOTAL		

☐ Check enclosed   ☐ Bill my credit card   ☐ Ship to address(es) on back

Name _____

Address _____

City _____ State _____ Zip _____

Daytime Phone _____

Card No. _____ Expiration _____

Cardholder Name _____

Signature _____

Make checks payable to Lightworks.com, then mail or fax your order to:

Lightworks.com
P.O. Box 1342
Morton Grove, IL 60053
Fax: 847-966-6535

Or place your order on our website:
www.lightworks.com
Email: tma@lightworks.com
Phone: 847-966-1110

Check box on front and indicate alternative "Ship To" addresses below.

Time Zone Edition: ☐ Eastern ☐ Central ☐ Mountain ☐ Pacific
Name _____
Address _____
City_____State_____Zip _____

Time Zone Edition: ☐ Eastern ☐ Central ☐ Mountain ☐ Pacific
Name _____
Address _____
City_____State_____Zip _____

Time Zone Edition: ☐ Eastern ☐ Central ☐ Mountain ☐ Pacific
Name _____
Address _____
City_____State_____Zip _____

Time Zone Edition: ☐ Eastern ☐ Central ☐ Mountain ☐ Pacific
Name _____
Address _____
City_____ State_____Zip_____

Time Zone Edition: ☐ Eastern ☐ Central ☐ Mountain ☐ Pacific
Name _____
Address _____
City_____ State_____Zip_____

Printed in the United States
64347LVS00008B/150